Bibliographies of Modern Authors
ISSN 0749-470X
Number Seventeen

The Work of
ROSS ROCKLYNNE

An Annotated Bibliography & Guide

by
Douglas Menville

Edited by Boden Clarke

R. REGINALD
The Borgo Press
San Bernardino, California ◦ MCMLXXXIX

Library of Congress Cataloging-in-Publication Data

Menville, Douglas Alver.
    The work of Ross Rocklynne : an annotated bibliography & guide
/ by Douglas Menville ; edited by Boden Clarke.
        p. cm. -- (Bibliographies of modern authors, ISSN 0749-470X ;
no. 17)
    Includes index.
    ISBN 0-8095-0511-8 : $19.95. -- ISBN 0-8095-1511-3 (pbk.) :
$9.95
    1. Rocklynne, Ross, 1913-1988—Bibliography. 2. Science fiction,
American—Bibliography. I. Title. II. Series: Bibliographies of modern
authors (San Bernardino, Calif.) ; no. 17.
Z8750.33.M46 1989   88-34360
[PS3535.O297]
016.813'54--dc19   CIP

Produced, designed, and published by Robert Reginald and Mary A.
Burgess, The Borgo Press, P.O. Box 2845, San Bernardino, CA 92406.
Cover design by Highpoint Type & Graphics, Claremont, CA. Cover
photo courtesy of Keith Rocklin.

FIRST EDITION——December, 1989

CONTENTS

DEDICATION

INTRODUCTION:

A MAN FOR ALL MAGAZINES

There is one thing that must be insisted upon, and that is the centrality of Ross Rocklynne to science fiction at one stage of its development. It must be insisted upon because it has so often been lost sight of; his *representativeness* has simply not been recognized. In large part this has been due to a characteristic flaw in the scholarly and semi-scholarly studies of the history of science fiction and its past writers.

During the 1920s, '30s and '40s, the science-fiction field consisted almost entirely of what was published in pulp magazines; book-published science fiction was sparse, haphazard and atypical. But university scholars and the editors of academic presses cannot bring themselves to recognize the existence of the ephemeral, flimsy and now all-but-unobtainable magazines; and then, too, it seems likely that they are embarrassed by the vulgarity of *Planet Stories* and *Thrilling Wonder Stories* and by the necessity of constantly referring to such publications. The result is that the magazines have been assigned to a kind of intellectual limbo. Only books have the dignity and accessibility (for references must be given and must be checkable) that a professional-level scholarly study requires. Anyone who has tried to write an "entry" for an "Encyclopedia" or "Dictionary," or a "Handbook of Science Fiction" on some writer dating from the 1930s and '40s knows the frustration of trying to deal with this attitude...and knows his own eventual defeat. Several writers who were popular in the '30s, '40s and '50s have suffered neglect in the '70s and '80s because of this.

Ross Rocklynne is one of them. The huge and seemingly comprehensive *Twentieth-Century Science-Fiction Writers* (St. James Press, 1986, 2nd edition) grants the existence of only two books and two shorter pieces (of course published in book form) by Rocklynne; but in granting even that much (or that little), they have done better than the even larger *Dictionary of Literary Biography, Vol. 8: Twentieth-Century American Science-Fiction Writers* (Gale Research, 1981), which doesn't take cognizance of his existence at all!

This naturally strikes older readers and those who have made themselves familiar with the science fiction of the past as an inadequacy, a falsity, a downright injustice, because we have the impression that Ross Rocklynne was somehow central to science fiction, especially during the '40s. When we turn to our collections and bibliographies to test this impression, we make a rather unexpected discovery: it is even truer than we thought. Ross Rocklynne was not only one of the central names in the science fiction of the period, there is a sense in which his was *the* central name! The reader may smile...but nevertheless it is true. There were names that were more intensely famous but none that were more widely recognized. Ross Rocklynne had, consistently, a wider range of publication than any other writer during what it loosely called the Golden Age of Science Fiction (from the late '30s through the early '40s).

The magazine science fiction of the time—and to repeat, there was virtually no other kind—tended to segregate itself into three main groups. First, there was *Astounding Science-Fiction*, over which loomed the socratic titan John W. Campbell Jr., who had carefully nurtured into being a stable of writers: Robert A. Heinlein, A. E. van Vogt, L. Sprague de Camp, Isaac Asimov, Lester del Rey and Theodore Sturgeon. These writers were conscious of their positions as contributors to the one magazine in the field with any claim to intelligence and quality and were not eager to appear in the lesser magazines. When their stories did appear elsewhere, they were often *Astounding* discards; and one writer, A. E. van Vogt, simply destroyed the stories that Campbell rejected.

The second grouping was of the writers who filled the pages of the science-fiction magazines published by the pulp chains, such as Standard and Popular: *Startling, Thrilling Wonder, Future, Super Science, Astonishing* and *Planet*. These were men (and a few women) struggling to make a living in a highly competitive field at low rates who could do so only by producing material very quickly. They were not adverse to writing for the other kinds of pulps published by the chains—western, adventure, detective and mystery magazines. They looked upon *Astounding* as a prestige market that they could not hope to hit regularly, if they managed to hit it at all.

The third group was almost a world unto itself, its core consisting of what might be called the in-house writers of the Chicago-based *Amazing Stories* and *Fantastic Adventures*, edited by Raymond A. Palmer: Don Wilcox, Leroy Yerxa, David Wright O'Brien and (if my youthful judgment did not deceive me) the group's one distinctive talent, David Vern, better known to readers under his pseudonym David V. Reed.

One name appeared regularly in all these magazines: Ross Rocklynne. In this, he was not only unusual, he was unique. When we examine the work of the other large producers during this period, we find that this rather surprising statement is true. Edmond Hamilton did not appear in *Astounding* (or *ASF*, as it was affectionately called) at that time. Those who read that magazine exclusively, and there were many, would hardly have been aware of his existence.

Jack Williamson, an honored name in *Astounding*, did not appear in *Planet* or *Amazing*. Those who read *Amazing* exclusively, and there were many, might never have heard of him. Murray Leinster appeared in most magazines, but *Amazing* knew him not; and Frederick Arnold Kummer Jr. (an unknown name now, but he had fifteen stories published one year and sixteen the next) made only one appearance in *ASF* during his entire career, and that very early. It might be thought that the even more prolific Henry Kuttner (actually, the man-and-wife writing team of Kuttner and C. L. Moore) was just as ubiquitous as Rocklynne—and he was; but we are speaking here of name recognition, and Kuttner's habit of resorting to multitudinous pseudonyms prevented his name from being recognized in all the science-fiction neighborhoods where Rocklynne's was well known. Lewis Padgett and Lawrence O'Donnell were household names in *ASF*, but Henry Kuttner was only a casual acquaintance and even less well known in *Amazing* (one story, 1942).

In short, only Ross Rocklynne was equally at home in each of the three realms. He differed from the pulpeteers of the Standard and Popular chains in that he easily and habitually sold to *ASF*. He had, altogether, twenty-one stories in that idea-centered and science-oriented publication; and during the few years in which the bulk of those appeared, he had an almost equal number of stories in what would seem to have been that magazine's polar opposite: the action-centered and adventure-oriented *Planet Stories*, appearing in the first without any sense of high exclusiveness and in the second without slumming. A newsstand browser looking over a display of the colorful magazines on, let us say, some cold, sunny mid-November day in 1942 might have been first puzzled and then bemused and then...well, astonished, to see the same name in several competing publications, with a short story ("Interlude") in the handsome, dignified, large-sized *Astounding*; a short story in *Thrilling Wonder* ("Storm in Space"); another short story in the rather dismal-looking *Future* ("The Creator"); still another in the five-cent (or did it cost ten cents by this time?) *Astonishing* ("Abyss of Darkness"); and a *novel* ("Day of the Cloud") in *Startling Stories*! Somehow or another, Rocklynne had missed appearing in the November and December issues of *Amazing Stories*; but his was a familiar byline there all the same.

And this was the writer whom supposedly comprehensive scholarly works barely recognize, if they do at all, as having existed! Fortunately, Douglas Menville has undertaken to correct this situation by compiling the present bibliography.

Ross Rocklynne was born Ross Louis Rocklin in Cincinnati, Ohio, on February 21, 1913. He was the second of three children, a brother having preceded him by two years and a sister following in another two. Cincinnati must have been at that time a fairly good-sized town, and yet one imagines that it may still have been recognizable as the same town that Charles Dickens visited some seventy years before and which was one of the few places in America that he actually liked and lavishly praised.

One rather envies Ross his Cincinnati. And one envies him his having been born into a quieter and less cluttered time. He grew up during the 1910s and '20s, which, looking back from our present vantage point, seems, either falsely or truly, to have been a not very lively period, but one that was sunny and placid, like a long Sunday afternoon in fall. The Great War didn't touch him at all—he was too young; and no doubt by the time he had reached young manhood he accepted the Great Depression, as did so many others, as a more or less natural phenomenon, like an earthquake or a bad turn in the weather. He was not old enough to vote until 1934, at which time he was making himself felt as a citizen of the Republic of Fiction by turning out his first few stories.

His father, Francis Rocklin, was a home-town inventor, a basement and garage tinkerer with machines, a species of which the supreme type is Thomas Edison. I would like to have described him as an Eccentric Inventor, that figure so beloved in early science fiction, but Ross has objected to that description, and so I withold it out of deference to his filial feelings. The elder Rocklin spent much of his life trying to contrive a perpetual motion machine, but like all other researchers along that line, he was eventually defeated by the second law of thermodynamics. His most daring creation, though not one realized in his home workshop, was a novel kind of submarine: to escape German U-boats or other predators, it would extend its fins into wings and fly through the air like a flying fish. But he was unable to interest the government in this idea. It must not be thought, however, that all his ideas were ambitious but impractical. His younger son Ross assisted him with two inventions that were written up in *Popular Mechanics*: an upside-down pocket and a funnel-shaped keyhole...this last obviously being of incalculable benefit to anyone coming home drunk at three A.M.

Francis Rocklin's inventiveness appeared in one form or another in all three of his children. Ross's older brother also tried his hand at writing and had a few pieces published, including two stories: "Guts—and a Racquet" in *Sport Magazine* and the other in that Mount Parnassus of pulp periodicals, *Blue Book*. This story, "Storm Winds," was published under the by-line R. J. Rocklin, a biographical note explaining that the initials stood for "Rock John."

"Rock John Rocklin"—an admirable name for a pulp-magazine writer, unmistakably preferable to his actual name, Clyde Rocklin. Ross's baby sister Olive has worked on a broader front: a Los Angeles and Hollywood resident, she paints, sculpts, plays the piano, sings and acts.

During Ross's boyhood—which one imagines as composed mostly of scenes from the *Saturday Evening Post* covers of the period—there occurred a curious disjuncture: he somehow found himself at the age of twelve in a boys' home. It was evidently a superior boys' home, if one judges by the name, Kappa Sigma Pi, but still, it was a boys' home and he was there for five years.

He has mentioned only one notable thing that occurred during this long stay: a black janitor introduced him to science fiction. This would have been at the very beginning of magazine science fiction, the Hugo Gernsback era of *Amazing Stories*, *Amazing Stories Quarterly* and *Science Wonder Stories*, generous, large-sized, *thick* magazines, published at a time when a quarter bought a lot of reading matter. These magazines at first reprinted stories by H. G. Wells and Jules Verne; then, a little later, they introduced such new talents as David H. Keller, Jack Williamson and E. E. Smith. Ross recalls that the last "in August of 1928 had me raving inside with 'The Skylark of Space'"; and he recalls all three with more admiration and affection than he feels for any more recent name.

He became an avid reader, collector, hoarder of the magazines. And when he was finally back home again there occurred one of those incidents with which readers and collectors of the time were only too familiar. He had hidden his treasured magazines in a corner behind a piano. An uncle discovered them there and asked him, "Have you read these?" Naturally, he had and he said so; whereupon his uncle gathered them up and hauled them away—his nephew, having read them, would of course have no further use for them. This was not the first, the last nor the most important deprivation of Ross's life, but it was one of which the sting could still be felt half a century later.

It wasn't many years after this when he began supplying the field with his own fiction. His first published story was "Man of Iron," in the August 1935 *Astounding Stories*, already the best science-fiction magazine of the three in the field and the only one to pay a whole penny a word for fiction. He wrote other stories that were sporadically published during the rest of the decade, eleven in all; all but two appeared in *Astounding*.

The most striking of these was, I think, "The Men and the Mirror," in the July 1938 issue of the magazine. It seems to me a perfectly engineered piece of fiction, with a dramatic situation growing neatly and naturally out of a scientific problem (which is, in capsule form, Theodore Sturgeon's definition of science fiction). It's a quiet story, like most of Rocklynne's fiction, but it better deserves being accorded a classic status than many other noisier pieces of writing. Two men have landed on an asteroid—asteroids loomed large in the science fiction of the time—and find on that airless rock something that cannot be there: a human skeleton. Where could it have come from? Then, through some agency, they are shifted back to a atime in which the asteroid was still part of a larger, Earth-like planet. They have some hope of getting back to their own time—but know that one won't make it. For they now know where the skeleton came from. As it turns out, one of the pair is Deverel, a wanted criminal, whom the other man, Colbie, a policeman, has captured and is taking back to justice. The question: Will Deverel leave Colbie to die? The answer: This was the third of six "problem stories" that Rocklynne wrote featuring Colbie and Deverel (although the names were sometimes changed for editorial reasons).

Nineteen forty was a watershed year for Rocklynne. During that year he moved to Los Angeles and had no fewer than thirteen stories published, more than during the entire decade of the '30s. He was determined to support himself by writing and, over the next few years, he achieved that very difficult feat, his stories appearing, as amply testified to in these pages, in every magazine in the field.

The best of these were in *Astounding*, including what is probably his most famous story, "Time Wants a Skeleton," in the June 1941 issue. It appeared surrounded by such classic works as "Slan," "Sixth Column," "Microcosmic God," "Nightfall," "Universe" and "Methuselah's Children," and yet it held, and still holds, its own. "It was irresistable," writes either Brian W. Aldiss or Harry Harrison, co-editors of *The Astounding-Analog Reader: Vol. 1* (1972), page 91, "and at least one young reader cherished it for many years as the best piece of science fiction he had ever read."

A few months earlier Ross had had another memorable story published, this one not in *ASF*. It was "Into the Darkness," in the June 1940 *Astonishing*, the first of four stories with sentient stars as characters (and you're probably mistaken if you think you know the source of that idea). These stories were later published as a novel called *The Sun Destroyers*, half of an Ace Double (1973).

The number of Rocklynne's stories lessened considerably after 1946, and in the first few years following 1950 they dwindled to a trickle and were gone. One might suppose that this was because of his momentary involvement in Dianetics, a "science of mind" devised by L. Ron Hubbard and John W. Campbell which ended, or put into abeyance, several other science-fiction careers. But in this case the supposition would be wrong. Actually, Ross had developed an extremely painful affliction of the face and jaw. Ross found that he could forget the pain only when involved in some physical activity or when socially engaged with others. When he was alone the pain tended to monopolize his attention and this made the lonely and reflective pursuit of writing very difficult, if not impossible. This was reason enough to surrender the calling...and of course one doesn't have to look far to find other practical reasons to give up a profession that offers no health care, no pension plan and no paid vacations. He supported himself for the next fifteen years by driving a taxicab about the streets of Los Angeles.

But if there were pressures away from writing, there were also pressures toward it; in 1967 he decided to make a fresh effort. He sat down and surprised everyone by turning out some stories that were very unlike anything he had written before, stories perfectly attuned to the Age of Aquarius. The best of these were probably "Ching Witch!" in the Harlan Ellison anthology, *Again, Dangerous Visions* (1972); "Randy-Tandy Man," in Terry Carr's *Universe 3* (1973); and "Emptying the Plate," in the April 1975 issue of *Fantastic Stories*. These first two stories, which appeared in publications that were among the most prestigious in the field, have an energy level much above that of his work of the Depression and war years. He had once again shown an enviable adaptability.

In person, Ross Rocklynne is now, and has been for some time, six feet two, a height topped with reddish hair that he admits is slightly touched with gray. He is solidly but not grossly built and could easily pass himself off as an ex-lumberjack or some other sort of outdoorsman, rather than as the city-dweller he has always been. Like most writers, from time to time during his life he has held various kinds of jobs—not only as a taxicab driver but as a clerk in clothing establishments and small retail stores; but unlike most writers, he was prolific enough and good enough to support himself entirely for some years with his pen and typewriter.

Ross was married in 1941 to Frances Rosenthal, a teacher of literature and creative writing and magazine editor who has since produced two books on writing under the name F. A. Rockwell. The marriage lasted seven years, and two good things, he says, came out of it: Keith Alan (born 1944) and Jeffrey David (born 1946). And Ross has been presented at one remove with three further good things: his grandchildren, by way of Jeffrey.

His mother and sister had followed him to Los Angeles in 1940. His mother was a lover of crossword puzzles and, in fact, had been working them since their very inception in the early part of the century. She lived to the age of 89, retaining to the end an interest in words, riddles and conundrums. My most vivid memory of her is her rapping her cane on the floor at her last birthday party and slyly demanding of the celebrants, "How long is a Chinaman?" and "Why is the Fourth of July?"

Ross's brother Clyde, who had abandoned writing for the steadier financial footing of real estate, is also gone. His sister Olive, very much present, has organized a novelty jazz band in which Ross sometimes plays the ukelele and mandolin with astonishing energy before groups large and small, in parks, convention halls and living rooms. He keeps in close contact with his family and a few good

11

friends, not the least of whom is Ms. Minnie Enos, who has often seemed to me the irrefutable proof that Dickens did not exaggerate when he created his heroines.

Ross has been forced to undergo far more than his rightful share of bodily disorders, not only the facial affliction mentioned before, but also—to cut the list short—angina pectoris and pulmonary edema. He bears these painful burdens with something of the stoicism of Job and with a good deal more cheerfulness and humor than was shown by that patriarch. He lives in a house that is rather ideally situated for him. It is not too far from the beach city of Santa Monica and even closer to one of the most pleasant areas of Los Angeles, Westwood Village. Oddly enough, he lives next door to a railroad line—which would be all right in itself if it were not for the unfortunate fact that he lives on the wrong side of the tracks. It is not unknown for a visitor, approaching his house from the direction of Westwood, to trip over one of the rails and sprawl full length in the iron-shod dirt. But the proximity of the line might be said to have benefited him in a publicizing way—although it's not a publicity he has sought: for the railroad, in gracious recognition of his presence, has placed in the road directly in front of his door a hexagonal metal sign bearing his initials: "R.R."

His home is not much cluttered with science fiction, his collection, mostly of his own work, being stored elsewhere. But he is in his own person a constant reminder of our science-fiction past, a living link with the Golden Age of Science Fiction and with the lively and somehow innocent age of the swarming pulp magazines...although, jaded and habituated as we are, we tend to forget this from time to time.

This was unexpectedly brought home to me by a recent experience. Ross and Minnie had just returned from Sacramento; while there, he had become acquainted with a young fan of his, an enthusiastic fourteen-year-old boy. This struck a chord with me, for I was reminded of something that had happened when I was that very same age and living in that same city. My brother and I were, as it happened, leaving Sacramento for Los Angeles; as we loitered about the station waiting for our bus to be called, my eye fell upon the cover of a magazine in a newsrack. It had a marvelous cover showing a blue rocketship swooping low over a city with guns blazing, the guns protruding from turrets that were notched in a convincing way for full mobility. It was a wonderful magazine, filled with exciting stories—"science-fiction" stories they were called—and I had to have it. I had to read those tales of life in the future and adventures on other planets; I had to read that "book-length novel" the cover illustrated. But my brother was strongly opposed to buying the magazine, saying, quite rightly, that the fifteen-cent cover price was just too much—it would be a disastrous drain on our financial resources. I'm afraid I threw a tantrum, even though I was all of fourteen; my last ever, I suppose and hope...but it worked: my brother gave in and the magazine became mine. I read it on the bus and it made the long trip south much shorter than it otherwise would have been, although all details of its contents faded from my memory as adolescence faded.

But I remembered the moment; so now, when Ross said that he had meant to send the young fellow in Sacramento a copy of his *Startling Stories* novel, "Pirates of the Time Trail," but had found that he had no copy, I decided to obtain it for him. I stopped in at Collectors Book Store in Hollywood and asked for the issue. A young man brought it out...and when I saw the cover, not just the memory of that Sacramento moment, but the very feelings I had had then, came flooding back in force. For here was that blue rocketship, with guns blazing! The magazine I had purchased then was the Fall 1943 issue of *Startling Stories*. The story I had read with such fascination was "Pirates of the Time Trail"...and its author, a man whom I had known for something like forty years but had somehow never identified as the author of a story that had helped bind me to science fiction with, as it were, hoops of steel, was...Ross Rocklynne.

—Arthur Jean Cox
Hollywood, California
February 1988

Note: Since this introduction was written, the science-fiction world has been saddened by the death of Ross Rocklynne on October 29, 1988. Instead of rewriting his introduction to reflect this fact, Mr. Cox has chosen to let it stand as written while Ross was still with us, and offers it as a memorial to our departed friend.

—Douglas Menville
July 1989

A ROSS ROCKLYNNE CHRONOLOGY

1913   Born February 21 in Cincinnati, Ohio, the second of three children of the marriage of Francis Joseph Rocklin and Rose Lena Vandermullen. His older brother, Clyde Rocklin, has been born in 1911. Ross lives with his parents in Cincinnati, attending school there and helping his father, a machinist, with his rather eccentric inventions in his spare time. Two of these are later written up in *Popular Mechanics*.

1915   His sister, Olive Rocklin, is born.

1925   As a result of his parents' separation, he is sent to live in a home for boys, Kappa Sigma Pi, where he goes to school and resides for five years. During this time he develops a passion for reading—Tom Swift, the Rover Boys, the Bible and especially the Tarzan novels of Edgar Rice Burroughs, introduced to him by a young schoolmate.

1928   He discovers science fiction with a vengeance through exposure to his first science-fiction magazine: the August issue of *Amazing Stories*, which features the first installment of E. E. Smith's "The Skylark of Space," as well as the first Buck Rogers story. He becomes an avid reader and collector of SF magazines.

1929   He writes some material for the school monthly—stories and jokes—and enters the cover story contest in *Science Wonder Stories* (November), his first attempt at science fiction. He doesn't win, but the winner, Charles R. Tanner, also lives in Cincinnati and later becomes a close friend. Ross returns home to live with his parents again.

1930   Continues to write SF stories and begins to submit them to magazines. Decides to alter his by-line from "Ross Rocklin" to the more sophisticated-appearing "Ross Rocklynne" and writes under this name for the rest of his career.

1934   Writes "Into the Darkness," the first of four stories in his "Darkness Series," and submits it to *Astounding Stories*, which rejects it.

1935   His story, "Man of Iron," is accepted and published in the August issue of *Astounding Stories*, thus becoming his first professionally published work of fiction.

1936   His second published story, "At the Center of Gravity," appears in the June issue of *Astounding*. This is the first of the "Colbie-Deverel" series, which will eventually encompass six stories. "Into the Darkness" is submitted to *Wonder Stories* and accepted, but is returned to him without payment when the magazine changes ownership. With the August issue, its title becomes *Thrilling Wonder Stories*.

1937   His career begins to pick up steam as he sells two more stories, both to *Astounding*. The first, "Water for Mars," appears as the cover story in the April issue, and his name appears on the cover of a science-fiction magazine for the first time.

1938   Sells his first story to *Amazing Stories* (June). "Escape Through Space" marks the beginning of his sales to many other SF magazines besides *Astounding*. Becomes friends with Charles R. Tanner, a fellow writer and SF fan who won the cover story contest back in 1929. Travels to other states, visiting Indianapolis, Clarksburg, Detroit and parts of Kentucky.

1939   "The Empress of Mars" appears as the third story in the first (May) issue of *Fantastic Adventures*. Attends the first World Science Fiction Convention, in New York City, and meets the greats of First Fandom. He becomes deeply involved in fandom himself, making friends with such fans and writers as Ray Bradbury, Forrest J Ackerman, Dale Hart, Charles D. Hornig and many others. Begins to contribute frequently to various fanzines, including the third issue of Ray Bradbury's famous publication, *Futuria Fantasia*.

1940   Sells 13 stories this year to various magazines, including "Into the Darkness," which is finally accepted by Frederik Pohl for *Astonishing Stories* (June). Also sells the first story in the "Sidney Hallmeyer" series to *Planet Stories* (Summer), his second sale to this magazine. Becomes a member of a fan group called "The Hell Pavers" and attends the second World Science Fiction Convention, in Chicago (Chicon). Moves to Los Angeles. His mother and sister follow later this year.

1941   Marries Frances Rosenthal on September 16. She is a writer, editor of *Writer's Digest* and teacher of literature and creative writing. She later authors two books on writing under the pen-name "F. A. Rockwell." Sells his first professional article, "Sweet and Harrow," to *Writer's Digest* (May). Continues to turn out a large volume of writing, including a venture into the western field (the first of several).

1942   His first two western stories are published, in *Fifteen Western Tales* (April) and *Western Short Stories* (October). Publishes his first story under a pseudonym, in order to have two stories appear in the same issue of *Planet Stories* (Summer): "As It Was," by "Carlton Smith."

1944   His first son, Keith Alan Rocklin, is born. Works as a story analyst for Warner Brothers Studios in Burbank, California, remaining there for four years.

1946   His second son, Jeffrey David Rocklin, is born.

1947   Is divorced from his wife and takes a job as a literary agent.

1948   Works at a variety of jobs (through 1949): sewing-machine salesman and repairman; machinist in a machine shop; art supplies salesman; building manager. During this two-year period, no new stories appear, as he is kept too busy to write consistently.

1950   Becomes interested in Dianetics and Eastern mysticism. Returns to writing and selling SF, with "Jaywalker," which appears in the third issue of *Galaxy Science Fiction* (December).

1951   A painful condition of the facial nerves contributes to his decision to stop writing completely awhile. His last published story before a 13-year hiatus is "Winner Take All," which appears in an original hardcover anthology, *Time to Come*, edited by August Derleth (1954).

1954   Supports himself primarily by dispatching and driving taxis in Los Angeles (through 1966).

1966   Visits his two sons in the Haight-Ashbury district of San Francisco and is influenced by the wild psychedelic culture of the '60s and by Marvel Comics. Begins to write again tentatively, with ten pages of what eventually becomes "Ching

Witch!," published by Harlan Ellison in 1972 as the second entry in his landmark anthology, *Again, Dangerous Visions.*

1967   Drops his interest in Dianetics and begins to write again, finishing "Touch of the Moon," which he submits to *Galaxy.*

1968   "Touch" is published in the April issue of *Galaxy,* marking a comeback which lasts for eight more years. Three other stories also appear in print this year.

1969   Six more stories are published through 1973, two of which are chosen for original hardcover anthologies: *Again, Dangerous Visions,* edited by Harlan Ellison (1972) and *Universe 3,* edited by Terry Carr (1973).

1973   His first two books are published in the same year, both paperback originals: *The Men and the Mirror* (Ace) and *The Sun Destroyers* (Ace Double). Contributes an introduction and story notes to the former.

1975   His final story (the 110th) is published: "Emptying the Plate," in *Fantastic Stories* (April). After this he retires from writing, largely due to illness, but pursues other interests, such as playing the ukelele and mandolin in a novelty jazz band organized by his sister.

1981   His first foreign-language book appears, in Italy: *Il Ladro delle Stelle,* a reprint of *The Men and the Mirror* (Libra Editrice). This is his only hardcover book to date. His last original piece of writing appears: an essay in a hardcover reprint edition, *Astounding Science Fiction July 1939,* edited by Martin H. Greenberg (Southern Illinois University Press). The essay is entitled, "On John W. Campbell, Jr. and Science Fiction."

1988   Celebrates his 75th birthday (February 21) with a big party at Kelbo's restaurant in West Los Angeles, attended by Forrest J Ackerman and his wife Wendayne, Ross's son Keith and his wife Victoria, writer and long-time friend Arthur Jean Cox, Roy Lavender, Minnie Enos, Douglas Menville, and other guests. Dies October 29 of heart complications. Is laid to rest at Hollywood Memorial Park. Rev. Harry Durkee presides over a short service in the Chapel of the Psalms, attended by close friends, neighbors, his sister and both his sons and their families. Forrest J Ackerman, who has known Ross for 49 years, gives the eulogy. Mourners include Douglas Menville, Minnie Enos, Arthur Jean Cox, Elmer Purdue, and Roy Lavender.

1989   His poem "The Departure" is published in *The Braille Mirror*, a
        monthly magazine published only in braille for the blind, as a
        posthumous tribute by the editor, Douglas Menville. The poem
        was written in 1975. *The Work of Ross Rocklynne: An Anno-
        tated Bibliography & Guide*, by Douglas Menville, the first
        comprehensive guide to the author's fiction, is published by
        Borgo Press.

A.

BOOKS

A1.   **The Men and the Mirror.** New York: Ace Books, February 1973, 208 p., paper. [collection]

This first (and only) collection contains six stories, five of which are reprinted from the pages of *Astounding Stories/Astounding Science-Fiction*, 1936-1946, and one from *Amazing Stories*, 1952. In his introduction to this collection, the author refers to these as "problem stories," in which the characters are forced to find the solutions to various scientific dilemmas in order to achieve their goals and/or preserve their lives. These stories—and especially the title story—were greatly admired by a youthful Isaac Asimov (see "Quoth the Critics").

CONTENTS: "At the Center of Gravity" (the author's second published story, 1936; see B2); "Jupiter Trap" (1937; see B5); "The Men and the Mirror" (1938; see B7); "They Fly So High" (1952; see B86); "The Bottled Men" (1946; see B76); and "And Then There Was One" (1940; see B12).   Together these stories comprise what the author called the "Colbie-Deverel" series, as they deal with the adventures of an interplanetary policeman, Lt. Jack Colbie, and his "friendly nemesis," space pirate Edward Deverel.   Two of the stories were rewritten and other character names used, for several reasons (see annotations for the individual stories), but the author claims that they all belong together as a series.   The sixth story in this collection, "And Then There Was One," is less closely related, but has a bearing on the premise of the first story.   Curiously, through either some bizarre editorial oversight (or even more bizarre editorial decision), the sixth story was not listed on the contents page and not included as a separate story! After the fifth story ends, on page 168, there is a short space and then the final story begins, without either title or story notes such as the author contributed to the other five stories.   The author also contributed an original introduction to this volume (see C14).

b.   as: *Il Ladro delle Stelle.* Bologna, Italy: Libra Editrice, 1981, 349 p., cloth.   The title translates as: *The Star Thief.*   This foreign reprint of *The Men and the Mirror* constitutes the author's sole publication to date in a hardcover edition, reflecting a regrettable oversight on the part of U.S. publishers. This volume contains an introduction by Ugo Malaguti (see G10) and a lengthy afterword by the editor and translator, Luigi Cozzi (see G11). It reprints only five of the "Colbie-Deverel" stories, and in a different order: "The Bottled Men," "They Fly So High," "At the Center of Gravity," "Jupiter Trap," and "The Men and the Mirror." (See individual story entries for the Italian titles used in this volume.) This book is No. 54 in a series of Italian SF classics called "Slan Fantascienza." [Italian]

SECONDARY SOURCES AND REVIEWS:

1. del Rey, Lester. *Worlds of If* 21 (July/August, 1973): 107-108.
2. Miller, P. Schuyler. *Analog Science Fiction/Science Fact* 92 (February, 1974): 172.

A2.   **The Sun Destroyers.** New York: Ace Double, March 1973, 156 p., paper. [novel]

This "novel," published as half of an Ace Double, with *A Yank at Valhalla*, by Edmond Hamilton, an old friend of the author's, is actually comprised of a series of four stories published separately in *Astonishing Stories*, 1940-42, and in *Imagination*, 1951. Together these stories form a connected narrative and are known as the "Darkness Series." The four stories are: "Into the Darkness" (see B17); "Daughter of Darkness" (see B33); "Abyss of Darkness" (see B45); and "Rebel of the Darkness" (the author's original title for this story, which was called "Revolt of the Devil Star" when it appeared in *Imagination* [see B83]). These stories were quite remarkable in their scope and originality, as they contained no human characters, but rather sentient stars and galaxies. They were among the most popular stories every published in *Astonishing* (see "Quoth the Critics"). This collection was originally scheduled for publication by Prime Press in the 1950s, but the company went out of business before it could be published.

SECONDARY SOURCES AND REVIEWS:

1. Briney, Robert. *Views and Reviews* 4 (Summer, 1973): 77-78.

B.

SHORT FICTION

B1. "Man of Iron," in *Astounding Stories* 15 (August, 1935): 94-99. The author's first professionally published work of fiction.

B2. "At the Center of Gravity," in *Astounding Stories* 17 (June, 1936): 67-77.

The first "Colbie-Deverel" story (see A1).

   b. *Exploring Other Worlds*, edited by Sam Moskowitz. New York: Collier Books, 1963, paper, p. 109-132.
   c. *The Men and the Mirror*, by Ross Rocklynne. New York: Ace Books, 1973, paper, p. 10-30.
  cb. as: "I Prigionieri di Vulcano," in *Il Ladro delle Stelle*, by Ross Rocklynne. Bologna: Libra Editrice, 1981, cloth, p. 167-196. [Italian]

B3. "Anton Moves the Earth," in *Astounding Stories* 18 (November, 1936): 124-149.

This was the author's longest story to date (13,000 words), making it what the pulps liked to call a "novelette."

B4. "Water for Mars," in *Astounding Stories* 19 (April, 1937): 10-46.

This story was featured on the cover of the magazine, marking the author's first cover story and the first time his name appeared on a science-fiction magazine cover.

B5. "Jupiter Trap," in *Astounding Stories* 19 (August, 1937): 46-61.

The second "Colbie-Deverel" story.

   b. *The Men and the Mirror*, by Ross Rocklynne. New York: Ace Books, 1973, paper, p. 31-57.

bb. as: "In Trappola du Giove," in *Il Ladro delle Stelle*, by Ross Rocklynne. Bologna: Libra Editrice, 1981, cloth, p. 197-250. [Italian]

B6. **"Escape Through Space,"** in *Amazing Stories* 12 (June, 1938): 30-42.

b. *Space Adventures* #10 (Spring, 1970): 108-119, 131.

B7. **"The Men and the Mirror,"** in *Astounding Science-Fiction* 21 (July, 1938): 74-98.

The third "Colbie-Deverel" story.

b. as: "Spegeln på Cyclops," in *Häpna!* 3 (October, 1956): 15-44. A Swedish science-fiction magazine. [Swedish]
c. *The Men and the Mirror*, by Ross Rocklynne. New York: Ace Books, 1973, paper, p. 58-104.
cb. as: "L'Occhio del Ciclope," in *Il Ladro delle Stelle*, by Ross Rocklynne. Bologna: Libra Editrice, 1981, cloth, p. 251-329. [Italian]
d. *Before the Golden Age: A Science Fiction Anthology of the 1930s*, edited by Isaac Asimov. Garden City, NY: Doubleday & Co., 1974, cloth, p. 954-985.
db. *Before the Golden Age: A Science Fiction Anthology of the 1930s, Book 3*, edited by Isaac Asimov. Greenwich, CT: A Fawcett Crest Book, August 1975, paper, p. 365-400.

B8. **"Who Was Dilmo Deni?"** in *Astounding Science-Fiction* 22 (November, 1938): 108-118.

B9. **"The Empress of Mars,"** in *Fantastic Adventures* 1 (May, 1939): 26-42.

The author's original title for this story was "A Warrior of Werg." A sequel, "Mission on Mars," was sold twice, to two different magazines, but was never published (see H22).

b. *Fantastic Adventures* 4 (October, 1942): 184-207.
c. *Fantastic Adventures Yearbook* 1 (1970): 68-91.
d. *Space Odysseys: An Anthology of Way-Back-When Futures*, edited by Brian Aldiss. London: An Orbit Book, Futura Publications, 1974, paper, p. 172-211.
db. *Space Odysseys: An Anthology of Way-Back-When Futures*, edited by Brian Aldiss. London: Weidenfeld & Nicolson, 1975, cloth, p. 138-171.

dc. *Space Odysseys: A New Look at Yesterday's Futures*, edited by Brian Aldiss. Garden City, NY: Doubleday & Co., 1976, cloth, p. 138-171.

dd. *Space Odysseys: A New Look at Yesterday's Futures*, edited by Brian Aldiss. New York: A Berkley Book, 1978, paper, p. 139-171.

B10. **"Pressure,"** in *Astounding Science-Fiction* 23 (June, 1939): 65-78.

b. *Imagination Unlimited: Science-Fiction and Science*, edited by Everett F. Bleiler and T. E. Dikty. New York: Farrar, Straus & Young, 1952, cloth, p. 95-118.

bb. *Imagination Unlimited*, edited by Everett F. Bleiler and T. E. Dikty. London: Bodley Head, 1953, cloth, p.   .

bc. *Imagination Unlimited*, edited by Everett F. Bleiler and T. E. Dikty. London: Mayflower-Dell, 1964, paper, p. 90-113.

B11. **"The Moth,"** in *Astounding Science-Fiction* 23 (July, 1939): 91-105.

b. *Astounding Science-Fiction July 1939*, edited by Martin H. Greenberg. Carbondale and Edwardsville: Southern Illinois University Press, 1981, cloth, p. 91-105. This hardcover volume featured an exact facsimile reproduction of the July 1939 *ASF*, which has been called "the first great issue edited by John W. Campbell," and "the spectacular opening salvo of the Golden Age of Science Fiction." In addition to the Rocklynne story, this issue also contained the first stories published in *ASF* by Isaac Asimov and A. E. van Vogt! This reprint volume also contains reminiscences by Asimov, van Vogt, and Rocklynne especially written for the book (for Rocklynne's essay, see C15).

B12. **"And Then There Was One,"** in *Astounding Science-Fiction* 24 (February, 1940): 53-77.

This story is considered by the author to belong in the "Colbie-Deverel" series, and is included as the sixth story in the collection *The Men and the Mirror* (1973), although it "departs from the cops 'n' robbers formula of the first five, but not too much. It is included because it lets you know why the premise of the first story is—*shudder*—scientifically incorrect."

B13. **"The Tantalus Death,"** in *Planet Stories* 1 (Spring, 1940): 61-70.

The author's original title was "Children of Tantalus."

B14. **"Trans-Plutonian Trap,"** in *Super Science Stories* 1 (March, 1940): 80-100.

B15. **"Unguh Made a Fire,"** in *Astounding Science-Fiction* 25 (April, 1940): 38-50.

This story was written in 1935.

b. as: "Unguh Machte ein Feuer," in *Utopia-Sonderband* 1 (Juni, 1956): 107-119. A German science-fiction magazine. [German]

B16. **"The Forbidden Dream,"** in *Planet Stories* 1 (Summer, 1940): 41-53.

The first of the "Sidney Hallmeyer" series, a group of five stories appearing only in *Planet Stories* and told in the first person by the main character, Sidney Hallmeyer, an interplanetary diplomat employed by the "Bureau of Transmitted Egos." When visiting a planet, Hallmeyer assumes a body of one of its inhabitants temporarily, to make his negotiations easier.

The noted science-fiction author, Chad Oliver, has written about this series: "[The Hallmeyer stories] are early examples of reshaping human beings to live on alien worlds. More than that, Hallmeyer was a person who *cared*. The stories have an atmosphere of compassion, of questioning basic values, of sadness. Indeed, there is an elegiac quality that pervades many of Rocklynne's better stories."

B17. **"Into the Darkness,"** in *Astonishing Stories* 1 (June, 1940): 44-63.

The first of the four stories comprising the "Darkness Series," this story was written in 1934 and scheduled to appear in *Wonder Stories* in 1936, after having been rejected by F. Orlin Tremaine for *Astounding*. However, *Wonder's* change of ownership in 1936 (upon which it became *Thrilling Wonder Stories*) caused the story to be returned to the author without publication or payment. He tried it with all the other SF editors around, but no one wanted to take a chance on a story without human characters. Finally, he heard of a new magazine, *Astonishing Stories*, edited by Frederik Pohl, and decided to try it there. Pohl loved it and bought it immediately, featuring it in the magazine's third issue.

Pohl's faith in the unusual story was richly justified, as the letter column of the next issue made it clear that "Into the Darkness" was one of the most popular stories ever published in that magazine (see "Quoth the Critics"). The fact that this story was written so long before its eventual publication also proves that the author's concept of sentient stars and galaxies was his own, and not derived from Olaf Stapledon's novel, *Star Maker*, as has been conjectured, since that work did not appear in print until 1937. Rocklynne has confirmed this.

b. *Futures Unlimited*, edited by Alden H. Norton. New York: Pyramid Books, 1969, paper, p. 125-153.

c. *The Sun Destroyers*, by Ross Rocklynne. New York: Ace Double, 1973, paper, p. 7-36.

d. *Classic Science Fiction: The First Golden Age*, edited by Terry Carr. New York: Harper & Row, 1978, cloth, p. 67-98.

e. *Isaac Asimov Presents the Great Science Fiction Stories: Vol. 2, 1940*, edited by Isaac Asimov and Martin H. Greenberg. New York: DAW Books, 1979, paper, p. 80-107.

f. *Yesterday's Tomorrows: Favorite Stories from Forty Years as a Science Fiction Editor*, edited by Frederik Pohl. New York: Berkley Books, 1982, paper, p. 9-31.

g. *Isaac Asimov Presents the Golden Years of Science Fiction*, edited by Isaac Asimov and Martin H. Greenberg. New York: Bonanza Books, 1983, cloth, Second Section, p. 80-107.

B18. "The Reflection That Lived," in *Fantastic Adventures* 2 (June, 1940): 42-50.

B19. "The Mathematical Kid," in *Amazing Stories* 14 (June, 1940): 86-98, 129.

The original title was "The World That Was a Mountain." A sequel, "Alphabet Scoop," was published in *Nebula Science-Fiction*, a Scottish SF magazine, in 1953 (see B94).

b. *Astounding Stories Yearbook* 1 (1970): 54-66, 114.

B20. "Prophecy of Doom," in *Future Fiction* 1 (July, 1940): 43-54.

B21. "The Man Who Never Lived," in *Amazing Stories* 14 (September, 1940): 70-82.

The original title was "The Strange Identity of Blake Harrison."

b. *Amazing Stories Quarterly* 1 (Spring, 1941): 70-82.

c. *Space Adventures* #9 (Winter, 1970): 118-130.

B22. "**Quietus,**" in *Astounding Science-Fiction* 26 (September, 1940): 86-97.

b. *Adventures in Time and Space: An Anthology of Modern Science-Fiction Stories*, edited by Raymond J. Healy and J. Francis McComas. New York: Random House, 1946, cloth, p. 641-654.

bb. *Selections from Adventures in Time and Space*, edited by Raymond J. Healy and J. Francis McComas. New York: Pennant Books, 1954, paper, p. 128-143.

bc. *Famous Science-Fiction Stories: Adventures in Time and Space*, edited by Raymond J. Healy and J. Francis McComas. New York: Modern Library, 1957, cloth, p. 641-654.

bd. *Adventures in Time and Space: An Anthology of Science-Fiction Stories*, edited by Raymond J. Healy and J. Francis McComas. New York: Ballantine Books, 1975, trade paper, p. 641-654.

c. as: "Ausklang," in *Utopia-Sonderband* 1 (October 1955): 100-110. A German science-fiction magazine; this was its first issue. [German]

d. *Isaac Asimov Presents the Great Science Fiction Stories: Vol. 2, 1940*, edited by Isaac Asimov and Martin H. Greenberg. New York: DAW Books, 1979, paper, p. 191-204.

e. *Isaac Asimov Presents the Golden Years of Science Fiction*, edited by Isaac Asimov and Martin H. Greenberg. New York: Bonanza Books, 1983, cloth, Second Section, p. 191-204.

B23. "**The Gods Gil Made,**" in *Unknown* 4 (November, 1940): 68-81.

B24. "**Atom of Death,**" in *Planet Stories* 1 (Winter, 1940-41): 46-52.

The editors evidently wanted this to be an early example of minimalist fiction, as the author's original title was "The Molecule of Death."

B25. "**The Vanishing Witnesses,**" in *Fantastic Adventures* 3 (January, 1941): 62-75, 143, 144.

B26. "**Collision Course,**" in *Super Science Stories* 2 (January, 1941): 8-23.

B27. "**Exiles of the Desert Star,**" in *Planet Stories* 1 (Spring, 1941): 80-95.

The second story in the "Sidney Hallmeyer" series. The original title was "Last of the Star Empire."

B28. **"The Immortal,"** in *Comet Stories* 1 (March, 1941): 4-16.

   b. *Tomorrow's Universe: A Science Fiction Anthology*, edited by H. J. Campbell. London: Panther Books, 1953, cloth, p. 116-139.

   c. *Future Science Fiction* 1 (November, 1954): 27-39. An Australian science-fiction magazine.

   d. as: "Ewigkeit," in *Utopia Science-Fiction Magazin* 1 (#6, 1956): 72-83. A German science-fiction magazine. [German]

B29. **Big Man,"** in *Amazing Stories* 15 (April, 1941): 70-87.

   b. *Fantastic Stories* 19 (December, 1969): 104-121.

B30. **"Mutiny Aboard the 'Terra,'"** in *Planet Stories* 1 (Summer, 1941): 80-94.

The author's original title was "Exiles of the Planetoid."

B31. **"Time Wants a Skeleton,"** in *Astounding Science-Fiction* 27 (June, 1941): 9-49.

Perhaps the author's best-known and most ingenious story, it appeared as the cover story of this issue of *ASF*. An instant favorite, it has been reprinted many times. The author's original title was "The Skeleton on Ten-Oh-Seven."

   b. *The Astounding-Analog Reader, Volume One*, edited by Harry Harrison and Brian W. Aldiss. Garden City, NY: Doubleday & Co., 1972, cloth, p. 116-167.

  bb. *The Astounding-Analog Reader, Book One*, edited by Harry Harrison and Brian W. Aldiss. London: Sphere Books, 1973, paper, p. 142-198.

   c. as: "Der Ring aus der Vergangeheit" ("The Ring from the Past"), in *Comet Sonderband* 1 (Januar, 1978): 87-114. A German science-fiction magazine. [German]

   d. *Isaac Asimov Presents the Great Science Fiction Stories: Vol. 3, 1941*, edited by Isaac Asimov and Martin H. Greenberg. New York: DAW Books, 1980, paper, p. 149-202. In his portion of the introduction to this story, co-editor Greenberg erroneously calls it "one of the four that constitute his 'Darkness' series..." It is not part of this series (see A2).

e. *Isaac Asimov Presents the Golden Years of Science Fiction,
    Second Series*, edited by Isaac Asimov and Martin H.
    Greenberg. New York: Bonanza Books, 1983, cloth, p. 149-
    202.

f. *The Mammoth Book of Golden Age Science Fiction: Short Nov-
    els of the 1940s*, edited by Isaac Asimov, Charles G. Waugh
    and Martin H. Greenberg. London: Robinson, 1989, paper,
    p. 7-59.

fb. *The Mammoth Book of Golden Age Science Fiction: Short Nov-
    els of the 1940s*, edited by Isaac Asimov, Charles G. Waugh
    and Martin H. Greenberg. New York: Carroll & Graf, Pub-
    lishers, 1989, paper, p. 7-59.

B32. "The Voice," in *Thrilling Wonder Stories* 21 (October, 1941):
      86-95.

B33. "Daughter of Darkness," in *Astonishing Stories* 3 (November,
      1941): 68-85.

   b. *The Sun Destroyers*, by Ross Rocklynne. New York: Ace
      Double, 1973, paper, p. 37-81.

      The second of the four stories comprising the "Darkness Series."
      This story was also scheduled to be reprinted in the third issue
      of *Bizarre Fantasy Tales* (1971), but the magazine was discon-
      tinued.

B34. "The Wicked People," in *Super Science Stories* 3 (February,
      1942): 96-108.

B35. "The Electrical Butterflies," in *Fantastic Adventures* 4 (March,
      1942): 46-59.

   b. *Fantastic Stories* 20 (August, 1971): 84-97.

B36. "Varmints' Pay," in *Fifteen Western Tales* 2 (April, 1942):
      112-116, 118-126, 128, 129. [western story]

      This was the author's first sale of a story not science fiction or
      fantasy, and the first of a small number of stories sold to the
      western pulps. The author's original title for this story was
      "Backtrail Triggers."

B37. "Task to Lahri," in *Planet Stories* 1 (Summer, 1942): 2-19.

      The third story in the "Sidney Hallmeyer" series.

b. *Tops in Science Fiction* 1 (Spring, 1953): 58-75.

B38. **"As It Was,"** by "Carlton Smith," in *Planet Stories* 1 (Summer, 1942): 82-89.

This was the first story published by the author under a pseudonym (other than the one he adopted by changing the spelling of his last name from "Rocklin" to "Rocklynne"), used so that two of his stories could appear in the same issue of *Planet*. He used this pseudonym only once more, for the story "Pumpkin Eater" (see B74). The original title was "The Primordial Puddle."

B39. **"Return from Zero,"** in *Super Science Stories* 4 (August, 1942): 130-146.

B40. **"Jackdaw,"** in *Astounding Science-Fiction* 29 (August, 1942): 61-74.

b. *The Best of Science Fiction*, edited by Groff Conklin. New York: Crown Publishers, 1946, cloth, p. 764-785.
bb. *The Best of Science Fiction*, edited by Groff Conklin. New York: Bonanza Books, 1963, paper, p. 419-440.

B41. **"No Town for a Tinhorn,"** in *Western Short Stories* 5 (October, 1942): 85-100. [western story]

Original title was "Hole Card Turnabout."

B42. **"The Day of the Cloud,"** in *Startling Stories* 8 (November, 1942): 15-89.

This was the author's longest work to date, the lead novel (45,000 words) in this issue. In his *Annotated Guide to Startling Stories* (Starmont House, 1986), Leon L. Gammell calls this story "Better than average for this period." Original title was "In the Day of the Cloud."

B43. **"The Creator,"** in *Future Fantasy and Science Fiction* 3 (December, 1942): 62-72.

b. *Future Science Fiction* 5 (October, 1959): 93-107.

B44. **"Storm in Space,"** in *Thrilling Wonder Stories* 23 (December, 1942): 90-103.

The author claims this is a kind of prequel to "Water for Mars" (see B4).

B45. **"Abyss of Darkness,"** in *Astonishing Stories* 4 (December, 1942): 86-100, 102-106, 108-110.

The third of the four stories comprising the "Darkness Series."

   b. *The Sun Destroyers*, by Ross Rocklynne. New York: Ace Double, 1973, paper, p. 83-112.

B46. **"Interlude,"** in *Astounding Science-Fiction* 30 (December, 1942): 67-75.

B47. **"Backfire,"** in *Astounding Science-Fiction* 30 (January, 1943): 34-43.

   b. *Omnibus of Science Fiction*, edited by Groff Conklin. New York: Crown Publishers, 1952, cloth, p. 100-117.
  bb. *The Omnibus of Science Fiction*, edited by Groff Conklin. New York: Bonanza Books, 1980, cloth, p. 100-117.

B48. **"For Sale—One World,"** in *Super Science Stories* 4 (February, 1943): 11-27.

B49. **"Telecotes' Owlhoot Tutor,"** in *New Western* (1943): [western story]

The author's original title for this story was "Black Rider of the Telecotes."

B50. **"Slaves of the Ninth Moon,"** in *Planet Stories* 2 (March, 1943): 100-117.

The fourth story in the "Sidney Hallmeyer" series.

B51. **"The Sandhound,"** in *Planet Stories* 2 (May, 1943): 38-52.

The first of two stories featuring a Robin Hood-like character called "The Sandhound." The sequel, "The Sandhound Strikes," also appeared in *Planet* (see B61).

B52. **"Warrior Queen of Lolarth,"** in *Amazing Stories* 17 (May, 1943): 88-137.

B53. "**Exile to Centauri,**" in *Thrilling Wonder Stories* 24 (August, 1943): 13-48.

B54. "**Pirates of the Time Trail,**" in *Startling Stories* 10 (Fall, 1943): 15-91.

Another long story, the author's second longest to date and the lead novel (44,000 words) in this issue. In his *Annotated Guide to Startling Stories* (Starmont House, 1986), Leon L. Gammell calls this story "Well written and fast-paced, with a catastrophic climax worthy of anything ever dreamed up by old Doc Smith."

B55. "**The Powerful Pipsqueak,**" in *Amazing Stories* 17 (September, 1943): 158-170.

B56. "**Beyond the Boiling Zone,**" in *Startling Stories* 10 (Winter, 1944; actually December, 1943): 79-88.

B57. "**Intruders from the Stars,**" in *Amazing Stories* 18 (January, 1944): 44-100.

    b. *Science Fiction Adventures Classics* (unnumbered; actually #27) (November, 1973): 6-17, 20-30, 90-123.

B58. "**The Invisible Army,**" in *Thrilling Wonder Stories* 25 (Winter, 1944): 50-61.

B59. "**Victory Drums,**" in *Captain Future* 6 (Spring, 1944): 79-91.

B60. "**The Giant Runt,**" in *Thrilling Wonder Stories* 26 (Summer, 1944): 11-41.

Written from a two-page premise suggested by editor Oscar J. Friend.

B61. "**The Sandhound Strikes,**" in *Planet Stories* 2 (Spring, 1945; actually December-February, 1944-45): 2-23.

Sequel to "The Sandhound" (see B51). The author's original title was "Guardian of the Glass Empire."

B62. "**Venus Sky Trap,**" in *Thrilling Wonder Stories* 27 (Spring, 1945): 48-62.

B63. "**Cosmic Yo-Yo,**" in *Planet Stories* 2 (Summer, 1945): 97-106.

Original title was "Trailing the Asteroid."

B64. **"Rowboat Feud,"** in *Thrilling Western Stories* (May, 1945): .
[western story]

B65. **"The Bubble Dwellers,"** in *Planet Stories* 2 (Fall, 1945): 78-
109.

The fifth and final story in the "Sidney Hallmeyer" series.

B66. **"Gunfire in the Canyon,"** in *Famous Western* 7 (Summer, 1945):
53-61. [western story]

B67. **"The Last Outpost,"** in *Astounding Science-Fiction* 35 (July,
1945): 67-98.

B68. **"Gift Horse,"** in *Astounding Science-Fiction* 35 (August, 1945):
116-153.

B69. **"The Infidels,"** in *Astounding Science-Fiction* 36 (September,
1945): 63-83.

B70. **"The Diversifal,"** in *Planet Stories* 3 (Winter, 1945): 54-62.

   b. *Planet Stories* 4 (March, 1951): 62-71.
   c. *The Best of Planet Stories #1: Strange Adventures on Other
Worlds*, edited by Leigh Brackett. New York: Ballantine
Books, 1975, paper, p. 175-192.
   d. *Perry Rhodan #86*, edited by Forrest J Ackerman. New York:
Ace Books, 1976, paper, p. 112-132.

B71. **"Secret of Chamuki,"** in *Jungle Stories* 3 (Winter, 1945; actually November, 1945-January, 1946): 65-74.

The author's original title was "Gems of Chamuki."

B72. **"A Matter of Length,"** in *Astounding Science-Fiction* 36 (January, 1946): 118-137.

B73. **"Captives of the Weir-Wind,"** in *Planet Stories* 3 (Summer,
1946): 54-81.

Once again, the author had two stories in the same issue of
Planet, again using the pseudonym "Carlton Smith" for the second one (see B38 and B74).

B74. **"Pumpkin Eater,"** by "Carlton Smith," in *Planet Stories* 3 (Summer, 1946): 36-46.

This was the last time the author used this pseudonym.

B75. **"The Ice World,"** in *Thrilling Wonder Stories* 28 (Summer, 1946): 72-83.

Forrest J Ackerman, a long-time friend (since 1939) and some-time agent of the author, edited the *Perry Rhodan* series of paperback books for Ace. In dedicating *Perry Rhodan #25* (1973) to Ross, Ackerman wrote: "This American Edition is Dedicated to Ross Rocklynne, who has given us (amongst scores of memorable sf stories) *THE ICE WORLD* (1946)." When the British edition of *Perry Rhodan #25* was published (London: Orbit Books, 1977, paper), the word "American" in the dedication was replaced by the word "English."

B76. **"The Bottled Men,"** in *Astounding Science-Fiction* 37 (June, 1946): 66-94.

This story was considered by the author to be the fifth in the "Colbie-Deverel" series, although it was published *before* the *fourth* story ("They Fly So High") in the collection, *The Men and the Mirror* (see A1 and B86). About "The Bottled Men," the author states: "This story is Colbie-Deverel all over again, but I changed the names to protect the pages of *Astounding*. At least so I thought. The stories seemed to be from another era, not suited to the magazine's progression into better characterization and perhaps more mature plotting. With new characters I could produce side elements of conflict and do some whimsical stuff with characterization in the person of a lighthearted fake of a villain named Gull Norse."

b. as: "Männen i Flaskan," in *Häpna!* 3 (June, 1956): 21-50. A Swedish science-fiction magazine. [Swedish]

c. *The Men and the Mirror*, by Ross Rocklynne. New York: Ace Books, 1973, paper, p. 127-158.

d. as: "Ades: Nella Zona Bollente del Sole," in *Il Ladro delle Stelle*, by Ross Rocklynne. Bologna: Libra Editrice, 1981, cloth, p. 21-128. [Italian]

B77. **"Extra Earth,"** in *Startling Stories* 14 (Summer, 1946): 88-97.

B78. **"Six Tuesdays,"** in *Planet Stories* 3 (Fall, 1946): 85-93.

B79. **"The Good Egg,"** in *Thrilling Wonder Stories* 29 (Fall, 1946): 37-45.

B80. **"Giant of Ganymede,"** in *Amazing Stories* 20 (December, 1946): 36-50.

  b. as: "El Gigante de Ganimedes," in *Los Cuentos Fantasticos* #6 (Septiembre 15, 1948): 4-20.
  c. *Space Adventures* #13 (Spring, 1971): 60-73, 130.

B81. **"Distress Signal,"** in *Planet Stories* 3 (Spring, 1946-47): 35-43.

  Original title was "Smoke Signal."

B82. **"Jaywalker,"** in *Galaxy Science Fiction* 1 (December, 1950): 51-62.

  According to the author, editor H. L. Gold assigned Theodore Sturgeon to rewrite this story, which appeared in the third issue of *Galaxy*.

  b. *Galaxy Reader of Science Fiction*, edited by H. L. Gold. New York: Crown Publishers, 1952, cloth, p. 84-94.
  c. *First Step Outward*, edited by Robert Hoskins. New York: A Dell Book, 1969, paper, p. 70-84.
  d. This story was also adapted as an episode of the NBC science-fiction radio series, *X Minus One*, in 1956 (see E1).

B83. **"Revolt of the Devil Star,"** in *Imagination Stories of Science and Fantasy* 2 (February, 1951): 6-31.

  The author's original title was "Rebel of the Darkness," as this is the fourth and final story in the "Darkness Series." Editor William Lawrence Hamling cut 4,000 words and retitled the story for the lead spot in this issue.

  b. as: "Rebel of the Darkness," in *The Sun Destroyers*, by Ross Rocklynne. New York: Ace Double, 1973, paper, p. 113-156. For its inclusion as a chapter in this novelization of the "Darkness Series," the original title and missing 4,000 words were restored.

B84. **"Out of the Atomfire,"** with Bryce Walton, in *Future Combined with Science Fiction Stories* 2 (May, 1951): 9-33.

The author states: "I originally wrote this as a 10,000-word story which I handed over to Bryce Walton, who rewrote and expanded it." Original title was "Prisoners of the Iron Atom."

B85. "Slave Ship to Andrigo," in *Planet Stories* 5 (July, 1951): 4-22.

Original title was "Mission to Andrigo."

B86. "They Fly So High," in *Amazing Stories* 26 (June, 1952): 64-74.

This story was considered by the author to be the fourth "Colbie-Deverel" tale. He explains: "A fourth Colbie-Deverel was written after 'The Men and the Mirror' appeared. It was called 'The Outlaw Strider.' Mr. Campbell of *Astounding* quickly turned it down and I agreed with him. I waited an excessively long time before I rescued the scientific idea in the story. I deliberately used the same formula, kept 'Colbie' under another name, and used a Gurdjieff-like individual for the 'outlaw'; then cut the story to short-story length. 'They Fly So High' was supposed to be the first story in a series of four ('Nearly Reach the Sky,' 'Then Like My Dreams,' 'They Fade and Die'), but this project died when I gave up writing for a number of years."

b. *Fantastic Stories* 17 (January, 1968): 82-93.
c. *The Men and the Mirror*, by Ross Rocklynne. New York: Ace Books, 1973, paper, p. 109-126.
d. *The History of the Science Fiction Magazine, Part 3: 1946-1955*, edited by Michael Ashley. London: New English Library, 1976, cloth, p. 191-204.
db. *The History of the Science Fiction Magazine, Part 3: 1946-1955*, edited by Michael Ashley. Chicago: Contemporary Books, 1977, paper, p. 191-204.
e. as: "Tra gli Anelli di Saturno," in *Il Ladro delle Stelle*, by Ross Rocklynne. Bologna: Libra Editrice, 1981, cloth, p. 131-164. [Italian]

B87. "Courtesy Call," in *Startling Stories* 26 (July, 1952): 120-128.

B88. "Interplanetary Tin Can," in *Science Fiction Adventures Magazine* (first series) 1 (November, 1952): 44-56.

This story was sold to the Swedish magazine *Häpna!*, but the author has no proof that it was ever published there.

B89. "The Chuckliner," in *West* 78 (January, 1953): 66-71. [western story]

A new draft of a story originally submitted to a Street & Smith western pulp that folded.

B90. "Chicken Farm," in *Planet Stories* 5 (March, 1953): 34-42.

The author has called this his favorite story for *Planet*.

b. *Planet Stories* (British Edition) #10 (1953): 34-44.

B91. "Fulfillment," in *Startling Stories* 29 (April, 1953): 83-99.

B92. "Sales Talk," by "H. F. Cente," in *Planet Stories* 6 (July, 1953): 67-75.

This was the only story published under this penname, the only published pseudonym used by the author besides "Carlton Smith" (see B38 and B74). He humorously derived this name from his belief that he would receive only a half-cent per word for this story, although in fact he was paid a cent a word. This is a rewrite of a 1937 reject, "Infinity B.C."

B93. "The Big Tick," in *Cosmos Science Fiction and Fantasy* 1 (September, 1953): 121-128.

Originally written in 1948 as "Davidge's Watch."

b. *Cosmos* 1 (September, 1953): 121-128. An Australian science-fiction magazine.
c. as: "Etwas Stirbt," in *Utopia Science Fiction Magazin* #9 (1957): 52-58. A German science-fiction magazine. [German]

B94. "Alphabet Scoop," in *Nebula Science-Fiction* 2 (September, 1953): 54-72.

A Scottish science-fiction magazine. This was the author's first story to appear in a foreign publication before appearing in the U.S.

b. *Science Fiction Digest* 1 (Fall, 1954): 75-90. The editor of this reprint magazine, which only lasted two issues, misspelled the author's name as "Ross Rocklynn." This story was a sequel to "The Mathematical Kid," which appeared in *Amazing Stories* in 1940 (see B19). Editor Ray Palmer rejected the sequel in 1941; Rocklynne rewrote it in 1951, and his agent at the time, Forrest J Ackerman, placed it with *Nebula*.

B95. **"X Marks the Asteroid,"** in *Imagination Stories of Science and Fantasy* 5 (January, 1954): 66-91.

B96. **"Sorry, Wrong Dimension,"** in *Amazing Stories* 28 (March, 1954): 82-89.

    b. *Amazing Stories* (British Edition) 1 (1954): 81-89.

    c. *The Diversifier* 4 (March, 1978): 53-59. The story as a one-act play. (See also D10).

B97. **"Winner Take All,"** in *Time to Come: Science-Fiction Stories of Tomorrow*, edited by August Derleth. New York: Farrar, Straus & Young, 1954, cloth, p. 233-260.

This was the first story the author sold directly to an anthology. It has never appeared in an American magazine, although reprint rights were sold to a German science-fiction magazine, the title of which was unfortunately unknown to the author. This story was written as a dissenting, up-beat reply to the story, "Winner Lose All," a grim and pessimistic tale by Jack Vance which appeared in the December 1951 issue of *Galaxy* and was reprinted in Groff Conklin's anthology, *Omnibus of Science Fiction* (1952). Ross also had a story in that anthology—"Backfire" (see B47).

    b. *Time to Come*, edited by August Derleth. New York: A Berkley Book, December 1958, paper, p. 154-172.

    bb. *Time to Come*, edited by August Derleth. New York: Tower Books, 1965, paper, p. 170-192.

    bc. *Time to Come*, edited by August Derleth. New York: Pyramid Books, 1969, paper, p. 165-185.

A German edition of *Time to Come* was supposed to appear, according to Rocklynne, but he is uncertain whether it was ever published.

B98. **"Touch of the Moon,"** in *Galaxy* 26 (April, 1968): 126-147.

This was the author's first new story to appear after a hiatus of 13 years!

B99. **"Daisies Yet Ungrown,"** in *Galaxy* 26 (June, 1968): 58-71.

Original title was "Daisies As Yet Ungrown."

B100. **"Find the Face,"** in *Galaxy* 27 (September, 1968): 61-73.

Original title was "The Great Star Face."

B101. **"The Sound of Space,"** in *Fantastic Stories* 18 (October, 1968): 6-16, 146.

This story was written and submitted under the pseudonym "Crosly Conners," but appeared under "Ross Rocklynne."

B102. **"Moon Trash,"** in *Amazing Stories* 43 (January, 1970): 6-16, 29.

B103. **"The Ideas,"** with Edith Ogutsch, in *Witchcraft and Sorcery* 1 (January-February, 1971): 24-26.

Rocklynne claims that this story was actually written by Ms. Ogutsch, but that she asked him to put his name on the manuscript with hers in order to sell it. It worked. Ross also did some slight revising and submitted it to two advertising magazines, which rejected it, before selling it to *Witchcraft and Sorcery*.

B104. **"The Passing of Auntie Mat,"** in *Worlds of Fantasy* 1 (Spring, 1971): 120-134.

B105. **"The Lorn of Toucher,"** in *Witchcraft and Sorcery* 1 (May, 1971): 32-33.

B106. **"Ching Witch!"** in *Again, Dangerous Visions: 46 Original Stories*, edited by Harlan Ellison. Garden City, NY: Doubleday & Co., 1972, cloth, p. 10-26.

The editor thought so highly of this story that he placed it in the second spot in this prestigious anthology.

   b. *Again, Dangerous Visions I*, edited by Harlan Ellison. New York: A Signet Book, New American Library, 1973, paper, p. 12-28.
  bb. *Again Dangerous Visions: 46 Original Stories*, edited by Harlan Ellison. London: Millington, 1976, cloth, p. 10-26.
  bc. *Again, Dangerous Visions: Book 1*, edited by Harlan Ellison. London: Pan Books, 1977, paper, p. 12-28.

bd. *Again, Dangerous Visions: 46 Original Stories*, edited by Harlan Ellison. New York: Berkley Books, 1983, trade paper, p. 10-26.

B107. **"Fat City,"** in *Amazing Stories* 46 (September, 1972): 58-65, 129.

The author states: "The idea for this story came from a newspaper column of Bob Considine's. He gave me his written permission to use it. It was returned from a bunch of upper-class magazines before I gave in and tried Ted White at *Amazing*." Original titles were "A Crumb for Mr. Big" and "Mr. Uggridges Goes to Thinland."

B108. **"Randy-Tandy Man,"** in *Universe 3*, edited by Terry Carr. New York: Random House, 1973, cloth, p. 119-132.

b. *Universe 3*, edited by Terry Carr. New York: Popular Library, 1973, paper, p. 111-122.
c. as: "Monsieur Mic-Mac," in *Après Nous le Délire: Douze Univers en Folie (After Us, the Delirium: Twelve Mad Universes)*, edited and translated by Jacques Chambon. Belgium: Casterman, 1977, cloth, p. 33-49. [French]

B109. **"The Doom That Came to Blagham"** (Chapter 5 of *Othuum*, a round-robin novelette), in *Witchcraft and Sorcery* #10 (December, 1974): 16-20.

The author states: "Gerald Page of *Witchcraft and Sorcery*, about August of 1970, mentioned the possibility of five authors writing a novelette of the cosmic menace type. A 'round robin.' He asked me to find a 1960s-type writer who would be agreeable. David Gerrold agreed, thought it 'would be fun.' In March of 1971 Jerry sent me the first four chapters of *Othuum*. They were by Brian Lumley, David Gerrold, Emil Petaja, and Miriam Allen deFord. I wrote the concluding chapter five. *Othuum* was finally published in *Witchcraft and Sorcery* in December 1974."

B110. **"Emptying the Plate,"** in *Fantastic Stories* 24 (April, 1975): 24-47.

This is the author's last published story. His original title for it was "Some Crumbs from a Rich Man's Table." He also considered a title variant of the final published title: "I Empty the Plate."

C.

NONFICTION

C1. "Meet the Authors: Ross Rocklynne, Author of 'Escape Through Space,'" in *Amazing Stories* 12 (June, 1938): 6. [autobiography]

C2. "Introducing the Author: Ross Rocklynne, Author of 'The Empress of Mars,'" in *Fantastic Adventures* 1 (May, 1939): 85. [autobiography]

C3. "Meet the Authors: Ross Rocklynne, Author of 'The Mathematical Kid,'" in *Amazing Stories* 14 (June, 1940): 131. [autobiography]

C4. "Sweet and Harrow," in *Writer's Digest* 21 (May, 1941): 30-34, 47. [writing]

C5. "Science Fiction Simplified," in *Writer's Digest* 21 (October, 1941): 25-30. [writing]

C6. "Sunk! Saved!" in *Writer's Digest* 22 (December, 1942): . [writing]

C7. "The Story Behind the Story," in *Thrilling Wonder Stories* 23 (December 1942): 127-128. [autobiography]

   Rocklynne contributed a short piece on how he came to write "Storm in Space" (see B44), which appeared in this issue. He shared space in the magazine's regular column, "The Story Behind the Story," conducted each month by the editor, with Frank Belknap Long, explaining his John Carstairs story, "The Ether Robots."

C8. "PS's Feature Flash," in *Planet Stories* 2 (May, 1943): 106. [autobiography]

C9. "Meet the Author: Ross Rocklynne Brings Us Up to Date on the Facts of His Life," with Oscar J. Friend, in *Startling Stories* 10 (Fall, 1943): 125-126. [autobiography/biography]

Rocklynne and editor Friend collaborated on this updated biography, which includes a photo of Rocklynne. This issue featured Rocklynne's cover novel, "Pirates of the Time Trail" (see B54).

C10. "The Story Behind the Story," in *Thrilling Wonder Stories* 27 (Spring, 1945): 112. [autobiography]

In this issue, Rocklynne explains how he came to write "Venus Sky Trap," a short story (see B62). He shares the column with Jerry Sheldon, who talks about his novel, "Devils of Darkonia."

C11. "Introducing the Author: Ross Rocklynne," in *Imagination* 5 (January, 1954): 2, 151. Includes photo. [autobiography]

C12. "Introduction to 'Ching Witch!'" with Harlan Ellison, in *Again, Dangerous Visions: 46 Original Stories*, edited by Harlan Ellison. Garden City, NY: Doubleday & Co., 1972, cloth, p. 7-9. [autobiography]

In his introduction to Rocklynne's story, Ellison let the author speak for himself with a brief autobiographical piece that had originally been intended for L. Sprague de Camp's *Science-Fiction Handbook* (Hermitage House, 1953). Unfortunately, it arrived too late for inclusion in that book, and so was published in Ellison's anthology for the first time.

    b. *Again, Dangerous Visions I*, edited by Harlan Ellison. New York: A Signet Book, New American Library, 1973, paper, p. 7-11.
    c. *Again, Dangerous Visions: 46 Original Stories*, edited by Harlan Ellison. London: Millington, 1976, cloth, p. 7-9.
    d. *Again, Dangerous Visions: Book 1*, edited by Harlan Ellison. London: Pan Books, 1977, paper, p. 7-11.
    e. *Again, Dangerous Visions: 46 Original Stories*, edited by Harlan Ellison. New York: Berkley Books, 1983, trade paper, p. 7-9.

C13. "Afterword" [to "Ching Witch!"], in *Again, Dangerous Visions: 46 Original Stories*, edited by Harlan Ellison. Garden City, NY: Doubleday & Co., 1972, cloth, p. 26-27. [autobiography]

Rocklynne contributed this short autobiographical piece about how he came to write "Ching Witch!" as a result of a visit with his two sons in Haight-Ashbury in 1966.

b. *Again, Dangerous Visions I*, edited by Harlan Ellison. New York: A Signet Book, New American Library, 1973, paper, p. 28-30.

c. *Again, Dangerous Visions: 46 Original Stories*, edited by Harlan Ellison. London: Millington, 1976, cloth, p. 26-27.

d. *Again, Dangerous Visions: Book 1*, edited by Harlan Ellison. London: Pan Books, 1977, paper, p. 28-30.

e. *Again, Dangerous Visions: 46 Original Stories*, edited by Harlan Ellison. New York: Berkley Books, 1983, trade paper, p. 26-27.

C14. **"Introduction"** and Story Notes, in *The Men and the Mirror*. New York: Ace Books, 1973, paper, p. 7-9, 10, 31, 58, 109, 127.

The author contributed an introduction to this collection of his "Colbie-Deverel" stories, describing how they came to be written, plus individual short introductions to five of the six stories: "At the Center of Gravity," "Jupiter Trap," "The Men and the Mirror," "They Fly So High," and "The Bottled Men" (see A1).

C15. **"On John W. Campbell, Jr., and Science Fiction,"** in *Astounding Science Fiction July 1939*, edited by Martin H. Greenberg. Carbondale & Edwardsville: Southern Illinois University Press, 1981, cloth, p. 177-180. [anthology]

An original article commissioned by the editor for this hardcover facsimile reprint of the historic July 1939 issue of *ASF*, in which Rocklynne's story "The Moth" appeared (see B11). Rocklynne considered this essay to be "somewhat autobiographical, but largely in praise of Campbell."

D.

FANZINE CONTRIBUTIONS

NOTE: During his youth Ross Rocklynne was active in the world of science-fiction fandom and contributed many pieces of writing to various amateur and semiprofessional magazines called "fanzines." Thousands of these publications were produced by zealous fans and continue to be published today. Unfortunately, only a few of Rocklynne's contributions can be accounted for, and these are listed below, spanning four decades.

D1.   "The Great Question," in *Scienti-Snaps* 3 (February, 1940): 17-20. [article]

D2.   "The Best Ways to Get Around," in *Futuria Fantasia* 1 (Winter, 1940): . [article]

This article on methods of space travel used in the SF magazines appeared in the third issue of the legendary fanzine published and edited by Ray Bradbury. Only four issues were published. Bradbury and Rocklynne were friends and pen-pals for many years, and each thought highly of the other's work. In one issue of *Futuria Fantasia* Bradbury contributed a biographical paragraph about Rocklynne in which he stated that "Somehow I had imagined a Rocklynne with a sharp gaunted face and bulging muscles—I found, instead, a good example of what mite [sic] be called typical college species number 569Z, a cross between science and wit, well mixed and jelled in an Empire State-tall body."

D3.   "The Care and Coddling of Ideas," in *Nova* 1 (1942): 19-22. [article]

D4.   "Gostacus: Discii: Destimabat," in *The Fantasite* (May-June, 1943): . [article]

The author states: "I think the strange title [of this article] was a *Latinized* version of a short story Miles J. Breuer, M.D., wrote for *Amazing Stories* around 1928-29 [the actual issue was March, 1930]. The actual title was 'The Gostak and the Doshes.'"

D5. Letter to *Amazing Stories*, 1962, in which Rocklynne quite convincingly and at length defends Edgar Rice Burroughs in a rebuttal to a Charles Dixon, who had written a letter earlier stating his belief that Otis Adelbert Kline's Burroughs imitations were superior to the originals. This letter of Rocklynne's almost constitutes a short essay on the merits of Burroughs over Kline. It was submitted to *Amazing Stories* for publication in the magazine's letter column, but was never published. So it finally appeared in the fanzine *Shangri L'Affaires* #70 (January, 1965): 8-11.

D6. "Inside Ross Rocklynne," by R. L. Rocklin, in *Lore* 1 (November, 1965): 16-18. [autobiography]

An amusing autobiographical sketch written as though Rocklin and Rocklynne were two different people. It was composed for the third issue of Gerald Page's fanzine.

D7. "Dale Hart, the Valentine Lad" (March, 1968): 1-4. [obituary]

A typed obituary of a noted science-fiction fan and friend of Rocklynne's, written to be published in a fanzine, possibly *Locus*, but the author cannot recall whether it was ever published and has no record of it. However, it is included in this section rather than under "Unpublished Works," because Rocklynne seemed to feel that it definitely *was* published somewhere.

D8. "Oh, to Be Free, Free, Free in 2053: An Approximately Correct Report of the St. Louiscon," in *Conglomeration* #3 (November, 1969): 6-10. [article]

D9. "Answering Dis-service," in *Poetry Humor Magazine* 1 (1976): 10. [humorous poem]

A short humorous poem poking fun at telephone answering services. It apppeared in the second issue of this amateur poetry magazine.

D10. "Sorry, Wrong Dimension," in *The Diversifier* 4 (March, 1978): 53-59. [one-act play]

The author adapted his short story into his only published play. The original story appeared in *Amazing Stories* 28 (March 1954) (see B96).   This play was first performed at the Poet/Dramatist Workshop in Garden Grove, California, on April 24, 1977.

D11.   Autobiographical paragraph in *Fantasy Faire Program Book* (July 27, 28, 29, 1979): 14. [autobiography]

The author contributed a brief autobiographical sketch to this 18-page program book for a science-fiction and fantasy convention.

D12.   **"The Departure,"** in *The Braille Mirror* 64 (May, 1989):   87. [poem]

This poem, written in 1975, was published posthumously in a monthly magazine published only in braille, for the blind, and edited by the author of this bibliography.   This magazine, while available only by subscription from the Braille Institute of America, is a professional publication; however, I have included it in this section to avoid setting up a separate section for only two poems.   I am publishing this poem for the first time for two reasons: first, as a tribute to my friend Ross, who I know would have loved seeing it published; and two, because it is an excellent poem.

E.

RADIO PRODUCTIONS

E1.   "Jaywalker," a half-hour radio adaptation of this story from
       Galaxy Science Fiction 1 (December, 1950) (see B82), was
       aired on the NBC science-fiction program, *X Minus One*, on
       April 17, 1956. This was the 42nd show in the series. The
       story was adapted for radio by George Lefferts and the cast
       included Bob Hastings, Teri Keane, Raymond Everett John-
       son, Connie Lemke, and Eugene Francis.

F.

JUVENILIA

F1. **"The Greater Love,"** in *Oracle* (1931): .

A short story published in the high-school yearbook of Woodward High, Cincinnati, Ohio. This and the following two stories were among various pieces contributed under his real name, Ross Rocklin, to his high-school annual and other school publications. Records have survived of only these three efforts, written when the author was 18 years old.

F2. **"Writer's Racket,"** in *Oracle* (1931): .

F3. **"Mr. Corpse,"** in *Oracle* (1931): .

G.

ABOUT THE AUTHOR

G1. "Meet the Author: Six-Footer Ross Rocklynne Tells the Tall Story of His Life," by Oscar J. Friend, in *Startling Stories* 8 (November, 1942): 128-129. [biography]

Although the title of this piece sounds like an autobiography, Rocklynne's recollection was that editor Friend wrote it for him. This issue features Rocklynne's cover novel, "The Day of the Cloud" (see B42). This article also includes a pen-and-ink sketch of the author.

G2. "Ross Rocklynne," by Sam Moskowitz, in *Exploring Other Worlds*, edited by Sam Moskowitz. New York: Collier Books, 1963, paper, p. 107. [biography]

G3. [Introduction to] "They Fly So High," plus a Checklist of the Author's Works, by Michael Ashley, in *The History of the Science Fiction Magazine, Part 3: 1946-1955*, edited by Michael Ashley. London: New English Library, 1976, cloth, p. 191, 298-299. [biography]

   b. *The History of the Science Fiction Magazine, Part 3: 1946-1955*, edited by Michael Ashley. Chicago: Contemporary Books, 1977, paper, p. 191, 298-299.

G4. "Rocklin, Ross Louis," in *Contemporary Authors: A Bio-Bibliographical Guide to Current Authors and Their Works, Volumes 61-64*, edited by Cynthia R. Fadool. Detroit: Gale Research Co., 1976, cloth, p. 461. [bio-bibliography]

G5. "Rocklynne, Ross," in *The Encyclopedia of Science Fiction and Fantasy Through 1968, Volume 2: Who's Who, M-Z*, edited by Donald H. Tuck. Chicago: Advent:Publishers, 1978, cloth, p. 367-368. [biography]

G6. [Introduction to] "Into the Darkness," by Terry Carr, in *Classic Science Fiction: The First Golden Age*, edited by Terry Carr.

New York: Harper & Row, 1978, cloth, p. 63-67. [biography]

G7. **"Rocklynne, Ross,"** by John Clute and Peter Nicholls, in *The Science Fiction Encyclopedia*, edited by Peter Nicholls. London: Roxby Press, 1979, cloth, p. 506. [criticism]

   b. *The Science Fiction Encyclopedia*, edited by Peter Nicholls. Garden City, New York, 1979, cloth, p. 506. Published simultaneously in trade paperback.

G8. **"Ross Rocklynne,"** by R. Reginald, in *Science Fiction and Fantasy Literature, a Checklist, 1700-1974; with, Contemporary Science Fiction Authors II* (2 vols.), edited by R. Reginald. Detroit: Gale Research Co., 1979, cloth, Vol. 1, p. 446, Vol. 2, p. 1052. [bio-bibliography]

G9. **"Rocklynne, Ross,"** in *Who Goes There: A Bibliographic Dictionary*, edited by James A. Rock. Bloomington, IN: James A. Rock & Co., 1979, cloth, p. 124-125. [bibliography]

   A poorly done reference work, riddled with errors and omissions: e.g., the editor is unsure of Rocklynne's real name; although this book purports to be a "guide to the works of authors...who have published all or some of their work pseudonymously," it lists only one pseudonym for Rocklynne—"H. F. Cente"—omitting the two stories published under the pen-name "Carlton Smith."

G10. **"Introduzione"** ("Introduction") to *Il Ladro delle Stelle* (*The Star Thief*), by Ugo Malaguti, in *Il Ladro delle Stelle*, by Ross Rocklynne, edited and translated by Luigi Cozzi. Bologna: Libra Editrice, 1981, cloth, p. 5-16. (See A1b). [criticism]

G11. **"Postfazione: Ross Rocklynne: Settant'anni di Avanguardia"** ("Afterword: Ross Rocklynne: Seventy Years in the Vanguard"), by Luigi Cozzi, in *Il Ladro delle Stelle*, by Ross Rocklynne, edited and translated by Luigi Cozzi. Bologna: Libra Editrice, 1981, cloth, p. 333-349. (See A1b). [criticism]

G12. **"Rocklynne, Ross,"** by Chad Oliver, in *Twentieth-Century Science-Fiction Writers*, edited by Curtis C. Smith. New York: St. Martin's Press, 1981, cloth, p. 454. [bio-bibliography]

In reviewing this book for *Aboriginal SF* (May-June, 1987), Darrell Schweitzer states: "So Ross Rocklynne is the author of two books and two stray stories, right? No, the bibliography misses a good 90 percent of his work, including several novels, all of which remain unreprinted in 1940s and '50s pulp magazines." This book even got the title of one of the "two stray stories" wrong, calling it "Emptying the Place" instead of "Emptying the Plate" (see B110).

G13. "Rocklynne, Ross," in *The Writers Directory, 1984-86.* Chicago: St. James Press, 1983, cloth, p. 828. [bio-bibliography]

G14. "Rocklynne, Ross," in *The Science Fiction Source Book*, edited by David Wingrove. New York: Van Nostrand Reinhold, 1984, cloth, p. 222. [criticism]

G15. Synopses of stories by Rocklynne that appeared in *Fantastic Adventures*, in *The Annotated Guide to Fantastic Adventures*, by Edward J. Gallagher. Mercer Island, WA: Starmont House, 1985, paper, p. 1, 11, 14, 26-27, 39. [criticism]

G16. Synopses of stories by Rocklynne that appeared in *Startling Stories*, together with critical comments, in *The Annotated Guide to Startling Stories*, by Leon L. Gammell. Mercer Island, WA: Starmont House, 1986, paper, p. 15, 16, 52, 56, 76, 80. [criticism]

G17. "Rocklynne, Ross," in *The Writers Directory, 1986-88.* Chicago & London: St. James Press, 1986, cloth, p. 801. [bio-bibliography]

G18. "Rocklynne, Ross," by Chad Oliver, in *Twentieth-Century Science-Fiction Writers, Second Edition,* edited by Curtis C. Smith. Chicago & London: St. James Press, 1986, cloth, p. 611. [bio-bibliography]

G19. "Rocklynne, Ross," in *The Writers Directory, 1988-90, Eighth Edition.* Chicago & London: St. James Press, 1988, cloth, p. 804. [bio-bibliography]

G20. "Rocklynne, Ross," by Bradley Denton, in *The New Encyclopedia of Science Fiction*, edited by James Gunn. New York: Viking Penguin, 1988, cloth, p. 390. [criticism]

G21. "Obituaries: Ross Rocklynne," by Arthur Jean Cox, in *Locus, the Newspaper of the Science Fiction Field* 21 (December, 1988): 60-61. [obituary]

G22. "Obituaries: An Appreciation by Richard Lupoff," by Richard Lupoff, in *Locus, the Newspaper of the Science Fiction Field* 21 (December, 1988): 61. [obituary]

G23. "Obituaries: Ross Rocklynne," by Don D'Ammassa, in *Science Fiction Chronicle, the Monthly SF and Fantasy Newsmagazine* 10 (January, 1989): 14. [obituary]

G24. "Introduction: A Man for All Magazines," by Arthur Jean Cox, in *The Work of Ross Rocklynne: An Annotated Bibliography & Guide*, by Douglas Menville. San Bernardino, CA: The Borgo Press, 1989, paper, p. 5-13. [biographical introduction]

G25. The Work of Ross Rocklynne: An Annotated Bibliography & Guide, by Douglas Menville. San Bernardino, CA: The Borgo Press, October 1989, 70 p., cloth. Published simultaneously in trade paperback. [bibliography]

H.

UNPUBLISHED WORKS

NOTE: Through the graciousness of Ross Rocklynne's son Keith, I have been allowed to go through Ross' papers and have uncovered a great many manuscripts of unsold stories, articles and poems. Some of these are untitled, others are untitled and unfinished; but I have attempted to list here primarily those that seem to be titled and complete. Most of the entries are dated, as Ross kept meticulous records on the majority of his material; however, in a few cases I have had to guess at undated stories. I am fairly certain that they have been placed within the correct decade, at least. In some cases, the actual manuscripts were missing, but Ross had prepared descriptive index cards for the material, and I have worked from these. It is interesting to note that among these manuscripts are several in *genres* to which Ross never managed to sell: mysteries, adventure stories, romantic stories, articles on metaphysics and at least one mainstream story. It is of further interest to note that Ross employed three more pseudonyms for four of his unsold stories: Crosly Conners, Paul Cahendon and Floyd Vischner. None of these pen-names appeared on a published work. All of the following stories are science fiction unless otherwise noted, and all manuscripts are typed except for one holograph piece (so indicated). Pages given are manuscript pages, and word count is also given whenever specified by the author.

H1.   "Trial on Mars," 1932, 8,000 words, 11 p.

H2.   "A White Carnation and a Green Coat," c1932, 17 p. Unfinished. [romantic story]

H3.   "Time Lapse Evaders," 1934, 18,000 words, 36 p.

H4.   "I Am Elaine," c1939. The only mention of this story is in a letter to the author from his agent in 1939. It was apparently a fantasy story, intended for John Campbell's magazine *Unknown* but rejected. [fantasy]

H5. "**Whither Goest Thou?**" c1939, 5,300 words, 22 p. Submitted to *Scribner's* but rejected, this is a slice-of-life-type story. [mainstream]

H6. "**Land of the Blue-Painted Men,**" by "Paul Cahendon," 1930s, 11,000 words, 32 p. This was the author's first story to be submitted under a pseudonym. Although written during the 1930s, it was reworked and submitted in the 1960s under this pen-name, along with another story, "Egg and Apple." The author's first sale under a pen-name came in 1942, with "As It Was," by "Carlton Smith" (see B38). Neither of the "Paul Cahendon" stories sold.

H7. "**The Incredible Migration,**" 1940, 9,000 words, 33 p.

H8. "**The Southern Californian,**" 1945, 17 p. A humorous contemporary tale. [romantic story]

H9. "**The Big Freeze,**" 1947, 6,000 words, 19 p.

H10. "**Landing Leander,**" c1947, 4,000 words, 18 p. [romantic story]

H11. "**One More Summer,**" c1947, 5 p. [romantic story]

H12. "**Trouble Trip,**" c1947, 13,500 words, 40 p

H13. "**Flight from Fancy,**" 1947, 15 p. An essay on inventions predicted by science-fiction writers in books and magazines. Probably a rewrite of a much earlier, undated piece entitled "Man Goes to Mars" (see H46). [article]

H14. "**Sing a Song of Conquest,**" 1948, 6,000 words. This story was written for and sold to *Planet Stories* in 1948, but the magazine was discontinued in 1955, before the story appeared. The author felt that it "seemed too poor to attempt sale elsewhere."

H15. "**Flight Through Space,**" 1948, 3,300 words, 12 p.

H16. "**The Brooch,**" 1948, 4,500 words, 16 p. A romantic adventure tale with an historic setting. Probably intended for a magazine like *Blue Book* or *Adventure*. [romantic adventure]

H17. "**Death Lottery,**" 1949, 5,500 words, 24 p.

H18. "**Down His Alley,**" 1940s, 4,000 words. Unfinished.

H19. **"Fan-Author Questions,"** 1940s, 2 p. A humorous article on the questions science-fiction fans ask authors, written for a fanzine, possibly Ray Bradbury's *Futuria Fantasia.* [article]

H20. **"The Long Shot,"** 1940s, 2,900 words, 11 p. A horse-racing story. [mainstream]

H21. **"My Pal the Rat,"** 1950, 5,000 words, 25 p. This mystery story was sold in 1950 but was never published. In 1956 Ross noted that "Even the people who bought it are no longer known to the agent." In 1970 he rewrote it and submitted it to several mystery magazines, but without success.

H22. **"Mission on Mars,"** 1951, 9,000 words. This was a sequel to "The Empress of Mars" (see B9), which appeared in the first issue of *Fantastic Adventures* (May 1939). The sequel was purchased by FA but never published. It was eventually returned to the author, who tried it again, twenty years later, this time with *Witchcraft & Sorcery.* Again the story was purchased, but this time the magazine was discontinued before it could be published.

H23. **"5,000,000 Revolting Babies,"** 1951, 12 p. A whimsical fantasy about telepathic babies. Submitted to *This Week* Sunday supplement magazine.

H24. **"A Comedy of Odors,"** 1951, 20 p.

H25. **"Ten Minutes to Think,"** 1951, 12 p. A metaphysical SF tale.

H26. **"The Return of the Mad Professor,"** 1952, 4,000 words, 14 p.

H27. **"I Use Pain,"** by R. L. Rocklin, 1963, 5 p. This was one of several articles on pain and how to deal with it that Ross wrote and submitted to various magazines, including *Scientific American*, *Playboy*, and *Saturday Review*, all of which rejected them. He later combined the information in the articles into the preface of his book-length manuscript on the same subject entitled *What to Do About Pain* (see H40). [article]

H28. **"The Meaning of Pain,"** by R. L. Rocklin, 1963, 21 p. A longer article on the same subject as H27. [article]

H29. "**Flying Right,**" by "Floyd Vischner," 1965, 2 p. Unfinished. Ross' second unpublished pen-name.

H30. "**The Old Grey Dog,**" 1967, 3,300 words, 13 p. [adventure]

H31. "**What If You're in a Crowd?**" 1967, 3 p. Sent to and rejected by *Playboy* "in one week." [article]

H32. "**Egg and Apple,**" by "Paul Cahendon," 1968 (1930s), 4,500 words, 14 p. This story, the only other to use this pseudonym besides "Land of the Blue-Painted Men" (see H6), was "rewritten from a very old reject" and submitted to *Galaxy*. It was rejected again.

H33. "**A Gang for All Time,**" 1968, 1,700 words. Rejected by *Cosmopolitan* and other magazines. Rewritten in 1973 and sent to *Woman's Day*, but again rejected. [romantic story]

H34. "**Bar Sinister,**" 1968, 9,000 words, 33 p.

H35. "**The Voyage to Zero,**" 1968. No manuscript for this story could be found; however, the author left a plot synopsis on an index card. The story may not actually have been written.

H36. "**I Live Under the Blue Star,**" by "Crosly Conners," 1969, 1,800 words, 14 p. This was the third unpublished pseudonym used by Rocklynne. Another story, written in 1968 and submitted under this pen-name, was sold to *Fantastic Stories* ("The Sound of Space"); however, it appeared under the author's "real name"—Ross Rocklynne (see B101).

H37. "**The Magical Vac,**" 1970, 11,200 words. This story was started in 1948 under the title, "The Magical Golden Vac," but was not finished until 1970. It was rejected by Robert Hoskins, editor of the Lancer Books *Infinity* series, and later by *The Magazine of Fantasy & Science Fiction*. [fantasy]

H38. "**The Asteroid Murder Case,**" 1970, 13,000 words, 55 p. This hybrid story, part science fiction and part murder mystery, was written for and rejected by John W. Campbell, then editor of *Analog*, who said that his readers didn't like SF mystery stories. It was also rejected by *Galaxy*. Of all his unpublished stories, the author seemed to think that this one might have the best chance of revision and an eventual sale. [novelette]

H39. **"What You Can Do About Pain,"** by R. L. Rocklin, 1970. (See H27.)

H40. **What to Do About Pain,** by Ross Louis Rocklin, 1971, 113 p. A complete book-length manuscript based on the ideas contained in his earlier articles (see H27, H28, H39). [nonfiction]

H41. **"Timemobile,"** 1971, 7,400 words, 29 p. *Galaxy* magazine accepted and paid for this story in February 1971, but the editor delayed publication so long that the author requested it be returned to him. He finally received it back in December 1974.

H42. **"Ronicky: A Tale of the Cold Northwest,"** 1971, 7,000 words, 25 p. Despite the title, this is a science-fiction story and not a straight adventure tale.

H43. **"Hey There, You with the Galloping Nose,"** by R. L. Rocklin, 1985, 5 p. A short self-help article on how to deal with the common cold. [article]

H44. **"Adventure in Yellow,"** by R. L. Rocklin, c1980s, 14 p. Unfinished. An attempt at autobiography—the author chronicles various experiences as a driver for the Yellow Cab Co. in Los Angeles during the 1950s. There is some indication that he intended this eventually to become a complete book, as sections are divided into chapters. [autobiography]

The remaining story and article manuscripts are all undated. In a few cases I have attempted to guess at approximate dates, but these are only estimates.

H45. **"The Ship That Came from Space,"** c1930s, 5 p. The only holograph manuscript found among the author's papers.

H46. **"Man Goes to Mars,"** c1930s, 20 p. A long essay about predictions in science-fiction books and magazines, an earlier version of "Flight from Fancy" (see H13). [article]

H47. **"Shipboard Romance,"** 6,000 words, 23 p. [romantic story]

H48. **"Knot Binding,"** 8 p. A humorous satire on the publishing industry. [satire]

H49. "Court Fool," 2 p. Unfinished. [romantic story]

H50. "Pandora's Box," 30 p. Unfinished.

H51. "Doll House on Ceres," 2 p. Unfinished.

H52. "Into the Sun," 18 p. Unfinished.

H53. "The Hand and the Key," 7,000 words, 26 p. A supernatural horror story with an historical background. It might have been intended for *Weird Tales*. [horror]

H54. "A Fifth-Rate Psychic," by R. L. Rocklin, c1980s, 7 p. An article on the author's psychic abilities, probably intended for *Fate* magazine. [article]

H55. "Finger Sight," by R. L. Rocklin, c1980s, 14 p. An article on "seeing" with fingertips, probably for *Fate*. [article]

Finally, here is a group of short poems, mostly humorous. Rocklynne had only two pieces of verse published, one in an amateur magazine (see D9: "Answering Dis-service") and the other in a magazine for the blind (see D12: "The Departure").

H56. "Death of a Soldier," c1940s, 1 p.

H57. "My Friends Don't Send Me," 1961, 1 p.

H58. "Lament for Barney Joe," 1975, 1 p.

H59. "Grey Flannel Goof," 1975, 1 p.

H60. "Inside of Old Pokey," n.d., 1 p.

I.

MISCELLANEA

I1.   PSEUDONYMS. The pseudonyms used by Ross Rocklynne
        (itself a pen-name, as his real name is Ross Louis Rocklin)
        are: Carlton Smith (two stories: see B38 and B74); H. F.
        Cente (one story: see B92); Paul Cahendon (two stories, nei-
        ther published: see H6 and H32); Crosly Conners (two stories:
        one was unpublished [see H36]. The second story, "The Sound
        of Space," was written and submitted under the Conners
        pseudonym, but was published under the author's "real" name,
        Ross Rocklynne [see B101]); and Floyd Vischner (one story,
        unpublished and unfinished: see H29). The derivations of
        these pseudonyms are unknown, except for H. F. Cente. This
        was an attempt at humor, as Ross believed he would receive
        only a half-cent per word for this story. As it turned out, he
        received a cent a word.

I2.   SERIES AND SEQUELS. During his career Ross penned three
        very popular series. Two of these have been collected in
        book form.

The Colbie-Deverel Series:

        1.   "At the Center of Gravity" (1936)
        2.   "Jupiter Trap" (1937)
        3.   "The Men and the Mirror" (1938)
        4.   "They Fly So High" (1952)
        5.   "The Bottled Men" (1946)
        6.   "And Then There Was One" (1940)

These stories were collected in paperback by Ace Books in 1973 under
the title, *The Men and the Mirror*, the author's first book (see A1).
The stories were arranged out of chronological order as published at
the author's request. He was very displeased with the way this book
was handled, as the editors carelessly left out his story notes to the final story (as described in A1). The following notes were to have appeared before "And Then There Was One." For the benefit of Ross'

friends and fans, who may have been puzzled by this, here are his original comments, published here for the first time anywhere:

Sir Isaac Newton provided the idea. He already had worked out the problem of the hollow planet before I approached it in "At the Center of Gravity." My answer was wrong. A decision was made to set the record straight, even though no complaining remarks about my ancient error had come through. The ten little Indians implied in the title became six big businessmen having a bit of a go at each other under rather strange and, in a manner of speaking, revolutionary conditions. Again, a planet was tailored to fit the problem.

The Darkness Series:

1. "Into the Darkness" (1940)
2. "Daughter of Darkness" (1941)
3. "Abyss of Darkness" (1942)
4. "Rebel of the Darkness" ("Revolt of the Devil Star") (1951)

These stories were collected in paperback by Ace Books in 1973 under the title, *The Sun Destroyers*, the author's second book (see A2).

The Sidney Hallmeyer Series:

1. "The Forbidden Dream" (1940)
2. "Exiles of the Desert Star" (1941)
3. "Task to Lahri" (1942)
4. "Slaves of the Ninth Moon" (1943)
5. "The Bubble Dwellers" (1945)

These stories have never been collected into book form. All appeared in *Planet Stories* (see: B16, B27, B37, B50, B65). In addition, there are three stories with one sequel each:

1. "The Empress of Mars" (1939)
2. "Mission on Mars" (1951)

The sequel was twice purchased but never published (see: B9, H22).

1. "The Mathematical Kid" (1940)
2. "Alphabet Scoop" (1953)

See: B19, B94.

    1.   "The Sandhound" (1943)
    2.   "The Sandhound Strikes" (1945)

See: B51, B61.

I3.   **NOVELS.** Although the bulk of Rocklynne's work falls into the categories of short stories and novelettes, four rank as "novels" (over 30,000 words) and are worthy of separation from his shorter fiction. They are:

    1.   "The Day of the Cloud" (1942, 45,000 words)
    2.   "Warrior Queen of Lolarth" (1943, 30,000 words)
    3.   "Pirates of the Time Trail" (1943, 44,000 words)
    4.   "Intruders from the Stars" (1944, 34,000 words)

See: B42, B52, B54, B57. In literary parlance (as opposed to the terminology used by magazines), these would all fall into the category of "novella."

I4.   **CATALOGING.** In the Library of Congress classification scheme, Rocklynne's main entry is "Rocklynne, Ross, 1913- ," his permanent literature number is PS3535.O297, and his bibliography number is Z8750.33.

QUOTH THE CRITICS

"I particularly liked *The Sun Destroyers.*   It surely was unusual and unexpected."

—Ray Bradbury

[The editors at Ace Books played a bit loose with Bradbury's actual comment when they used it as a cover blurb on *The Sun Destroyers.* In the letter column of *Astonishing Stories*, "Viewpoints" (August 1940), Bradbury wrote: "I particularly liked Ross Rocklynne's 'Into the Darkness.' It surely was unusual and unexpected." At this time Bradbury was 19 years old and a year away from selling his first story.]

"I encountered Rocklynne's work late in the game, 1951, when I read with considerable awe, 'Revolt of the Devil Star' in the now defunct *Imagination: Stories of SF & Fantasy*, a story about sentient stars. It was well beyond the terms and intents of what was being written in the field.   It was—Ross will excuse the phrase, I hope—very *avant-garde*. It was also exquisitely written."

—Harlan Ellison

"I loved the story ['The Men and the Mirror']. It is a problem story, using authentic science...The time was to come when I was to try to write problem stories, but doing one as pure as 'The Men and the Mirror' isn't easy."

—Isaac Asimov

"When I reread 'Time Wants a Skeleton,' however, I suddenly felt all the old excitement. I tried for a long time to put my feelings into a phrase that wasn't a cliché and then gave up. The cliché it had to be. "I said, 'They don't write stories like that any more.'"

—Isaac Asimov

"['Time Wants a Skeleton'] was irresistable, and at least one young reader cherished it for many years as the best piece of science fiction he had ever read."

—Brian W. Aldiss and Harry Harrison

"Ross Rocklynne was one of the important authors of magazine science fiction's middle years...His works was [sic] of sufficiently high quality that L. Sprague de Camp wanted to include him as one of the 20 or so leading writers in the field for his *Science-Fiction Handbook* (1953)... Usually a careful craftsman, he wrote many types of science fiction: competent space operas, time-travel stories, effective mood pieces, scientific puzzle stories, detective stories, and yarns spun around the Big Idea. Typical of the latter was 'The Moth' (*Astounding*, 1939). Here—in 14 pages—he presented what John Campbell called 'a wholly new idea for a spaceship drive' and for good measure threw in a fairly sophisticated picture of competing corporations...Ross Rocklynne was never less than a capable storyteller. However, he tried to be more than that: he pushed himself instead of always taking the easy way. He was a major creator of the science fiction of the past, but he was also one of those who pointed the way ahead."

—Chad Oliver

"RR had one of the most interesting, if florid, imaginations of pulp writers of his time, and wrote very much better than most...he later made a formidable comeback with several stories in 1968, demonstrating that he had no difficulty at all in adjusting his narrative voice to the more sophisticated demands of the later period, as in 'Ching Witch!,' one of the most assured *tours de force* in Harlan Ellison's *Again, Dangerous Visions* (anth. 1972), an ironic tale about the curious morality of a man, the result of genetic engineering, who has a lot of cat in him."

—John Clute and Peter Nicholls

"A versatile and sometimes experimental writer, Rocklynne was one of the regular pulp magazine short fiction writers between 1935 and 1954, but the quality of his writing exemplifies how individual writers could transcend the medium. His stories are thoughtful and well written, often including an ingenious scientific idea..."

—Bradley Denton

"Ross Rocklynne grew up in that quieter time and has, by his own words, paid his dues...He is...with substantial glory, a fine writer who has come through all the years of his life with his talent intact..."

—Harlan Ellison

INDEX

"Daughter of Darkness," B33
"The Day of the Cloud," B42
"Death Lottery," H17
"Death of a Soldier," H56
"The Departure," D12
"Distress Signal," B81
"The Diversifal," B70
"Doll House on Ceres," H51
"The Doom That Came to Blagham," B109
"Down His Alley," H18
"Egg and Apple," H32
"The Electrical Butterflies," B35
"The Empress of Mars," B9
"Emptying the Plate," B110
"Escape Through Space," B6
"Etwas Stirbt," B93c
"Ewigkeit," B28d
"Exile to Centauri," B53
"Exiles of the Desert Star," B27
"Extra Earth," B77
"Fan-Author Questions," H19
"Fat City," B107
"A Fifth-Rate Psychic," H54
"Find the Face," B100
"Finger Sight," H55
"Flight from Fancy," H13
"Flight Through Space," H15
"Flying Right," H29
"For Sale—One World," B48
"The Forbidden Dream," B16
"Fulfillment," B91
"A Gang for All Time," H33
"Giant of Ganymede," B80
"The Giant Runt," B60
"Gift Horse," B68
"El Gigante de Ganimedes," B80b
"The Gods Gil Made," B23
"The Good Egg," B79
"Gostacus: Discii: Destimabat," D4
"The Great Question," D1
"The Greater Love," F1
"Grey Flannel Goof," H59
"Gunfire in the Canyon," B66
"The Hand and the Key," H53
"Hey There, You with the Galloping Nose," H43
"I Am Elaine," H4

ABOUT DOUGLAS MENVILLE

Douglas Alver Menville was born August 16, 1935 at Baton Rouge, Louisiana. He came to California in the late 1950s to attend the University of Southern California, finally getting his master's degree from the USC film school in 1959; his master's thesis was the first full-length critique of fantastic films ever written, later being published in book form by Arno Press (1975). For the next decade, he worked as a film editor, before being named Editor of *Forgotten Fantasy* magazine (1970), and co-Editor of Newcastle Publishing Co., Inc. (1971); he also served as Advisory Editor for three Arno Press reprint series between 1975-78. Among his many book-length projects are *Things to Come* (1977) and *Futurevisions* (1985) (two illustrated histories of the science fiction film), twelve anthologies of fantastic literature, and (as editor) ten books on the tarot and numerology for Newcastle Publishing Co. He currently edits *The Braille Mirror* for The Braille Institute of America in Los Angeles. This is his first monographic bibliography.

www.ingramcontent.com/pod-product-compliance
Lightning Source LLC
LaVergne TN
LVHW041207080426
835508LV00008B/848